Conversations with

MOTHER TERESA

A Personal Portrait of the Saint,
Her Mission, and Her Great
Love for God

Conversations with

MOTHER TERESA

A Personal Portrait of the Saint, Her Mission, and Her Great Love for God

Renzo Allegri

Translated by Marsha Daigle-Williamson, PhD

Published by The Word Among Us Press
7115 Guilford Drive, Suite 100
Frederick, Maryland 21704
www.wau.org

15 14 13 12 11   1 2 3 4 5

ISBN: 978-1-59325-190-1
eISBN: 978-1-59325-415-5

Cover design by John Hamilton Design
Cover photo © Dwight Cendrowski

Made and printed in the United States of America

Library of Congress Cataloging-in-Publication Data

Allegri, Renzo.
   [Madre Teresa mi ha detto. English]
   Conversations with Mother Teresa : a personal portrait of the saint, her
mission, and her great love for God / Renzo Allegri ; translated by Marsha
Daigle-Williamson.
      p. cm.
   ISBN 978-1-59325-190-1
   1. Teresa, Mother, 1910-1997. I. Teresa, Mother, 1910-1997. II. Title.
   BX4406.5.Z8A5413 2011
   271'.97--dc23
   [B]
                                    2011026643

Contents

INTRODUCTION

A little over one hundred years ago, on August 26, 1910, Mother Teresa of Calcutta was born—the woman who astonished and conquered the world through her love for the poor.

Thousands of events to commemorate and honor this sister, proclaimed "Blessed" by the Church in 2003, occurred. Dioceses, parishes, and even civil authorities, cultural associations, and non-denominational groups organized them spontaneously—not only in the Christian world but in the Islamic, Jewish, Hindu, Buddhist, Taoist, and Shintoist worlds as well. Mother Teresa is a universal, ecumenical figure who is loved by all. Even the media were fully involved in the chorus of celebration of Mother Teresa: articles in journals, radio and television documentaries, and books. I wish to make my contribution to this vast sea of publications with this book, *Conversations with Mother Teresa*.

This is not a biography of Mother Teresa, so it cannot be characterized as a historical account of her earthly life. It is rather a record—the record of a journalist who had the good fortune, for professional reasons, to meet with this extraordinary woman several times. I want to remember her by focusing attention primarily on her own words. Mother Teresa spoke very little. She was above all an icon. She transmitted thoughts and reflections in her own way. Her face, her smile, her deep wrinkles, her eyes, her hands and feet deformed by arthritis, her small bent-over figure, and her gait all told of her suffering, her pain, and her constant physical weariness from ceaseless labor. It also testified to her total, absolute, unconditional dedication to others, to the neediest people on earth.

Whenever circumstances forced her to express herself in words, Mother Teresa was always brief and concise. She spoke in a subdued, humble, and loving voice. Having interviewed her several times (and on some occasions with the specific goal of retelling her life), I had an opportunity to tape-record various conversations with her. Mother Teresa's words retell events, offer advice, and elicit reflection. However, precisely because they are the words of Mother Teresa, they take on an important and extraordinary value.

While I was organizing her statements from the various interviews I had done, I had the impression of reliving those meetings, of once again hearing the loving voice of Mother Teresa and seeing her face, her eyes. It was a wonderful feeling, but it immediately led me to reflect on the fact that it was not merely an impression but a reality because Mother Teresa is alive, more alive than when she was on this earth, and she is always close to people who think about her. I sincerely hope that whoever has the kindness to read these pages will experience her constant presence through her words.

Renzo Allegri

Chapter One

•

A SPECIAL RAPPORT

The title of this book, *Conversations with Mother Teresa,* reflects the extraordinary experiences I had with this woman of God.

Precisely because of their profession, journalists often find themselves in situations they never would have expected. For forty years I have been a special correspondent for large newspapers and have encountered a wide variety of people: artists, politicians, scientists, sports champions, film stars, saints, and assassins—a very diverse and unending gallery of famous people.

I have written many articles about these people, and I have even had "scoops," which are the boast of any newspaper. Today newspapers pay for scoops, and they pay a high price for them. In earlier days this kind of payment was rare. I was never paid anything for my scoops; I got them through my own hard work and primarily through a large dose of good fortune.

For example, I am passionate about classical music and have had a column for twenty-five years in one of the most widely read newspapers in Italy. I've been able to meet, interview, and visit with many great musicians and singers, such as Luciano Pavarotti and Placido Domingo. In 1973 Maria Callas, one of the most famous women in the world at the time, was directing the opera *I Vespri Siciliani (The Sicilian Vespers* by Verdi) in Turin for the opening of the *Nuovo Teatro Regio* (New Royal Theater). On the eve of the opening, more than two hundred journalists and television and radio reporters had arrived from all over the world. Everyone hoped to get a quote from the "divine Callas," but she did not speak to any of them. However, I had the good fortune of spending three hours doing a long exclusive interview in her hotel room. I've had other such experiences as well.

The odd thing is that when I try to recall all these scoops, I realize that they were not the result of my ability but primarily of good fortune. I have always been very fortunate in my profession—patient and fortunate. And this is exactly how things transpired for me with Mother Teresa as well.

Fifteen Years of Waiting

I first thought about trying to interview Mother Teresa in 1971. I was fascinated by the activity and charisma of this religious sister, who was at that time still little known in Italy. I was won over the first time I read an article about her, and I began to plan for a meeting. However, I did not want a simple and hasty interview but a long conversation so that I could tell about her life in detail. It was a presumptuous desire, but I did achieve it in 1986, fifteen years later. As always, good fortune was on my side on that occasion as well.

There was a certain kind of trust—I would dare say even a precious friendship—between Mother Teresa and me that permitted me to meet with her at different times, to have multiple interviews, to travel with her, to drive her around in my car, and to obtain favors that I would never have thought possible. For example, she was the godmother at the baptism of a daughter of a friend of mine, the singer Al Bano, and also at the baptism of quintuplets in Rome.

It was Bishop Pavel Hnilica, a Slovak bishop living in Rome, who introduced me to Mother Teresa. He was a friend who had helped her open some homes for the poor in Rome. One day after I had met her, the bishop confided in me that Mother Teresa, who was usually very reserved, especially with journalists, had spoken freely with me and considered me a kind of son. He wrote these thoughts in the preface to one of my books on Mother Teresa. I include his comments here because they are very precious to me:

About fifteen years ago, I introduced Mother Teresa to the journalist Renzo Allegri. In that first encounter in Rome between Renzo and the very humble but great sister, I was impressed by the atmosphere of trust that was immediately created between the two of them. I believe I am not exaggerating when I say that there was a true spiritual rapport between these two people that both surprised and pleased me. Confirmation of that particular impression was given to me by Mother Teresa herself when she later told me that she felt comfortable with Renzo and appreciated his discrete and fair manner of journalism. Anyone who was close to Mother Teresa knew very well that it was not easy for a journalist to approach this luminous and transparent figure who fled every kind of publicity, let alone receive such a compliment from her.

I have always felt, and continue to feel, a very great gratitude for the kindness that Mother Teresa showed me and that I certainly did not deserve. I am grateful for the interviews that she gave me, for the extraordinary things that she told me about her life and her work on behalf of the poor, and for the loving advice she gave me—which, unfortunately, I did not always guard as a treasure.

In this book I have sought to collect not only the precious words of Mother Teresa but also her gestures and actions that were often more eloquent than the words themselves.

Longing to Go Home

The year 2010 marked the hundredth anniversary of Mother Teresa's birth. She could still be among us: I know several people who were born in 1910 who are still alive. Essentially, she, too, is still alive, in a much better way than when she was on earth. She would often say, "Death is nothing more than passing from a difficult life of suffering to an existence full of love and joy in God." And she would say it with a tone that took one's breath away.

One day I asked her out of the blue, "Are you afraid of dying?" She had been in Rome for a few days. I had met with her a couple of times and dropped by to visit her again before returning to Milan. She looked at me as though she wanted to understand the reason I was asking the question. I thought perhaps I had made a mistake in bringing up the subject of death, so I tried to change the topic.

"You seem rested," I said. "You seemed very tired to me yesterday."

"Yes, I rested well," she replied.

"In the last few years, you have had surgeries that were rather delicate, like your heart surgery. You should take care of yourself and travel less."

"Everybody tells me that, but I need to think of the work that Jesus entrusted to me. When I am no longer of use to him, he will be the one to stop me."

Completely changing the subject, she asked, "Where do you live?"

"In Milan," I answered.

"When are you going back home?"

"I hope to return tonight," I said. "I want to catch the last plane so that I can be with my family tomorrow."

"Ah, I see that you are happy about going home and seeing your family," she said, smiling.

"I have been away almost a week," I said to explain my enthusiasm.

"Very good, very good," she added. "You are right to be happy. You are returning to your wife and children, your loved ones, and your home. Things should be that way."

She remained silent for a few moments and then proceeded to launch back into the subject:

Look, I would be as happy as you if I could say that tonight I would die. In dying, I, too, will be going home. I will go to heaven and will find Jesus. I have consecrated my life to Jesus. In becoming a sister, I became the bride of Jesus. See? I wear a ring on my finger like married women do. And I am married to Jesus. Everything that I do on this earth, I do out of love for him, so when I die, I will be going home, to my husband's home. In addition, up there in heaven, I will also find all my loved ones. Thousands of people have died in my arms. For over forty years now, I have dedicated my life to the sick and dying. My sisters and I have gathered thousands and thousands of dying people off the streets, especially in India. We have brought them into our houses and helped them to die in peace. Many of these people expired in my arms while I was smiling and stroking their trembling faces. When I die, I will meet all those people again. They are waiting for me there. We loved each other in those difficult moments and have continued to love each other in our remembrance. Who knows what kind of party they might throw when they see me? How can I possibly fear death? I desire it and wait for it because finally, I will be able to go home.

I had never heard Mother Teresa speak so long and with such enthusiasm. Generally, in interviews, and even in conversation, she was concise and gave quick, brief answers. On this occasion, in order to answer my odd question, she had begun an authentic conversation, and while she was saying these things, her eyes sparkled with a serenity and a joy that was astounding.

•

Chapter Two

A DIMINUTIVE WOMAN
IN LOVE WITH GOD

On September 13, 1997, Mother Teresa's body was laid in a tomb in the heart of Calcutta. It was located on the ground floor of the motherhouse of the Missionaries of Charity, the religious community she founded in 1948 at the beginning of her ministry to the poorest of the poor.

It is a very simple tomb that remains there even after October 19, 2003, when she was proclaimed "Blessed" by Pope John Paul II. It is simple and made of concrete, without any decoration except a marble plaque. Below the cross at the top of the plaque, a verse from the Gospel of John is carved on the marble tombstone that summarizes the spirit of service of Mother Teresa's life: "Love one another as I have loved you (St. John 15:12)." Underneath the verse is the inscription "Mother Teresa 8.26.1910–5.9.1997, our dearly beloved Mother Foundress."

Among the People She Loved

The tomb is in a room that once was the dining room for the sisters. The large room has windows looking out on one of the busiest streets in Calcutta, Lower Circular Road, which is full of the city's poor. The deafening roar of traffic, the smell of smog, the stench of overflowing sewers, and the humidity of the seasonal rain enter into that room from the outside. This is the Calcutta that Mother Teresa loved: the Calcutta of the poor, of all kinds of people—the sick, the handicapped, the downtrodden.

These people, individually and in small groups, continue to enter that room throughout the day and stand before that tomb. They pray according to the religious customs of India; they speak to the mortal remains of that sister as if she were there to listen to them. Some of them make physical contact, leaving a flower or tenderly caressing the marble plaque.

It was not easy for the Missionaries of Charity to obtain permission to house Mother Teresa's body. Indian law prohibits people from keeping a body in a residential dwelling. However, the government made an exception for the diminutive saint of Calcutta. There is no more appropriate place for her eternal repose than this house where she worked for half a century among the people she loved.

Mother Teresa was one of the most well-known women in the world. History will certainly always remember her as one of the key religious figures of the Catholic Church in the second half of the twentieth century. She did her work without offices, palaces, multiple homes, secretaries, or cell phones—always in the streets. Mother Teresa lived, like those who assisted her, in poverty. It was therefore fitting that after her death, she returned to rest alongside the noisy street in the heart of Calcutta, in the midst of the people who have nothing.

The extraordinary adventure of Mother Teresa began precisely in that street, with all the appearance of being a foolhardy or mad scheme. She left behind what people would consider "reasonable" plans and abandoned herself to divine recklessness.

Only since her death, and especially after her beatification, do people now understand that her activity was a rock-solid act of faith in the gospel, an immense gesture of love. Mother Teresa, who was thirty-six years old when she decided to begin her ministry to the poorest of the poor, was in love—literally in love—with Jesus, and like all who are in love, she had acted on impulse, following the leading of her heart.

That love never diminished, and Mother Teresa continued to live like a person in love. Even though many years have passed since her death, she remains the symbol of the highest kind of generosity and altruism, the kind of virtue that ennobles humanity. Popes, heads of state, kings, government ministers, artists, intellectuals, politicians, and large groups of people from all races, religions, and ideologies admired her and bowed before her when she was alive, and they continue to do so now.

The Nobel Peace Prize

It was often said, "Mother Teresa is an angel." As Prime Minister of India Indira Gandhi once remarked, "In front of her, we all feel small and ashamed of ourselves."

The world has honored her with the most prestigious kinds of recognition. In 1962 India bestowed on her the Padma Shri Award, one of the highest honors from that republic. That same year the Philippine government awarded her the Ramon Magsaysay Award for peace and international understanding, which is considered to be the Asian Nobel Prize.

In 1971 Pope Paul VI awarded her the Pope John XXIII Peace Prize. In 1973 she was the first recipient of the Templeton Prize for Progress in Religion for her religious work, a prize presented to her by the prince of Edinburgh, Prince Philip. That prize was voted on unanimously by a board of ten representatives from various religious groups throughout the world, and she was selected from among two thousand candidates of various nationalities and religions. In 1975 she received the Ceres Medal from the United Nations Food and Agriculture Organization (FAO) for her exemplary love and concern for the hungry and the poor of the whole world. In 1978 she was awarded the Balzan Prize for promoting humanity, peace, and brotherhood among peoples.

The Nobel Peace Prize was given to her in 1979. After this prestigious recognition, many other awards followed, including the highest civilian honor in India, the Bharat Ratna (1980), the U.S. Presidential Medal of Freedom (1985), and the Congressional Gold Medal from the U.S. Congress (1997).

Proclaimed "Blessed" by the Church

There was perhaps no person in the twentieth century who was more celebrated and praised. Always humble and reticent, she continued to repeat with profound conviction, "I am nothing."

But God knew her heart. At her death he received her into his heavenly kingdom while the Church, only five years after her death, proclaimed her "Blessed." That solemn ceremony occurred on October 19, 2003, in St. Peter's Square, with overflowing crowds of the faithful from all over the world. Pope John Paul II celebrated the Mass. He was already quite ill, but he wanted to proclaim the sanctity of the nun whom he had esteemed and admired so much. He was suffering from Parkinson's disease, which impeded his speech, so he had the reading of the homily delivered by his concelebrator, Msgr. Leonardo Sandri. In his sermon the pope described Mother Teresa as a "courageous woman, . . . an icon of the Good Samaritan," adding, "Not even conflict and war could stand in her way." She had "chosen to be not just the least but to be a servant of the least." He invited everyone to "praise the Lord for this diminutive woman in love with God, a humble Gospel messenger and a tireless benefactor of humanity. In her we honor one of the most important figures of our time. Let us welcome her message and follow her example" (Pope John Paul II, Homily on the Beatification of Mother Teresa of Calcutta, October 19, 2003).

•

Chapter Three

A Ten-Year Wait

Journalists are generally interested in a topic or a personality that is relevant. When something happens that piques people's interest, off go the journalists to do interviews or write articles.

For me, this is not the way it happened with Mother Teresa. It was not an assignment from the newspaper I worked for that got me interested in her. It was the woman herself and her activities that aroused my curiosity.

Pope Paul VI's Admiration

The first time I heard the name of Mother Teresa of Calcutta mentioned was in 1971. On January 6 she came to Rome to receive the Pope John XXIII Peace Prize from Pope Paul VI. This was a new prize instituted by the pope that year, and it was prestigious precisely because he had instituted it. In addition, the prize included 15 million lire, which was a large sum at that time.

The newspapers reported the event but without much fanfare because Mother Teresa was still not well-known in Italy. The brief report, however, attracted my attention. I was amazed that Pope Paul VI would have chosen someone who lived and worked in India as the initial recipient of a prestigious prize. There had to be a special reason. So I read the official citation for the prize that the pope himself had written:

With great pleasure we award you the first Peace Prize in honor of Pope John XXIII. The prize was instituted to celebrate the World Day of Peace 1971 and is given on Epiphany in the presence of the diplomatic corps attached to the Holy See and the members of the Roman Curia. We have instituted this prize to honor the memory of our venerable predecessor, Pope John XXIII, and to promote the cause of peace and encourage all those throughout the world who dedicate their lives to helping people in body and spirit. Because of the unforgettable memory of our pilgrimage to India, we invoke from the depths of our heart all the divine graces upon the work of charity that you generously carry out every day, and we impart our apostolic benediction upon you. (Pope Paul VI, January 6, 1971, Vatican City)

I read and reread his words. Despite the solemn style of the Curia, one could perceive the profound admiration that the pope had for this sister. At the time the Church was still somewhat closed in on itself, and the pope never expressed himself too enthusiastically. However, I could tell from his words that he was very struck by what this woman was doing.

As Pope Paul VI explained in his speech, this was the first time the prestigious award was being given. For that very reason, he had wanted to select an exceptional, extraordinary person to hold up as an example to the world. So he chose this humble sister who was working in India.

The Gift of a Lincoln

Popes know that whatever they write will become part of history, so they are extremely prudent about what they say. Their writings are always measured, controlled, and carefully weighed, so in the end, less is said than might have been said. Because of that, Pope Paul VI's words really struck me. He pointed to Mother Teresa as an example for everyone in the world who "dedicates their lives to helping the poor in body and spirit." He indicated that the woman was absolutely wonderful, that she was a living saint, and that all Christians should take her as a role model. He spoke these words despite the fact that the powerful Roman Curia would perhaps never have approved such a laudatory declaration about a living person.

I discovered later that Pope Paul VI had admired Mother Teresa for a long time. He had met her in 1964 during his trip to India, as he noted in his remarks during the ceremony. He had gone to India to close the 38th International Eucharistic Congress that was being held in Bombay (now Mumbai). He had wanted to meet Mother Teresa on that occasion because he had already heard about her.

At the end of their meeting, he demonstrated his esteem and admiration with an unusual, odd gesture that got the attention of the press. A wealthy American industrialist had given the pope a very beautiful white automobile with red seats—a Lincoln that was worth thousands of dollars. At the end of the Eucharistic Congress, when he was about to leave Bombay, Pope Paul VI said, "We donate our white automobile to Mother Teresa to help her in her global mission of love."

From December 1964 on, after he had been pope for only a year and a half, Pope Paul VI demonstrated appreciation for this unusual sister who was dedicated to the poor in India.

Dying with Dignity

A few months after becoming aware of the awarding of that Peace Prize, I came across some articles from Calcutta that concerned Mother Teresa and her work. The author of the articles was reconstructing the history of Mother Teresa's work in India. He spoke of her help to the poorest of the poor, and in particular of the home that she had opened to assist the dying. This very unusual and humanitarian undertaking astounded me.

I knew that Calcutta was a very large city with around eleven million inhabitants, where misery seemed to have no limits, and poor people were dying on the sidewalks of the streets completely abandoned. The article emphasized that Mother Teresa had organized this Home for the Destitute Dying at a time—from 1953 to 1954—when the situation in that city had become even more dire.

At that time, the usual crowd of destitute people and vagrants was increased by thousands of Pakistani refugees and by tens of thousands of displaced persons who had lost everything in one of the many terrible cyclones that periodically hit the southwestern coast of Bengal. All these people were wandering around starving and at risk of disease, falling to the ground exhausted. Many of them died in the street.

Mother Teresa wanted to help them because she suffered deeply when she saw those people dying alone in the streets. She wanted them to be able to die in a clean bed with someone alongside them who would be concerned for them. "They are children of God. They should die with dignity and with a smile on their lips," she said. That was her reason for building a hospice for the dying. Every morning Mother Teresa and her young sisters went around the city to gather up the people who were dying on the sidewalks. They would bring these people home to this small hospital, bathe them, lay them in bed, and help them until their dying breath.

Reading about this work made me wonder. It was a marvelous thing, but it was bewildering as well. The sister who had conceived this idea was taking care of people who, in the eyes of the world, did not even exist—the poor and, on top of that, the poor who were dying.

Mother Teresa was doing this for them so that they could "die with dignity." There were no babies being saved, with their whole lives ahead of them, or even young people who, with help, could become useful members of society. These people were old, and many were consumed by leprosy—human wreckage, so to speak. To prolong their lives even for one day served no purpose except perhaps to make them suffer more. But this sister reasoned differently. For her, this "human wreckage" consisted of human beings, children of God, her most beloved brothers and sisters, and she wanted them to leave this world "with dignity," with the assurance that someone loved them.

Incredible! This particular concept made such an impression on me that I continued to reflect on it. I asked myself how and why this nun could have ever had such a thought enter her mind. I found her enterprise extremely humanitarian and decent, even poetic— like sublime poetry that comes from the wellsprings of life.

Using Feet and Knees

Mother Teresa came to Milan in 1973. She was invited by the Pontifical Institute for Foreign Missions to participate in a youth rally for missions. The youth of that region responded enthusiastically, and a crowd of ten thousand people gathered around the cathedral. Mother Teresa was in the front. It is cold in Milan in October, but she was wearing only her usual white sari with a thin wool sweater and coarse sandals of thick leather.

The organizers of the rally had invited her to speak before the youth paraded through the city. She climbed the platform and simply said, "Let us each do our part. Use your feet, and I will use my knees. While you walk through the city, I will pray for you." The youth began their march, and Mother Teresa went into a church near the cathedral square to pray and remained there until the demonstration was over.

The next day she was received at City Hall by the mayor of Milan, who awarded her the Ambrogino d'oro, a medal given to well-deserving people. The master of ceremonies pointed out, "Look, it's made of gold." Mother Teresa commented, "Well, then, this medal should have been given to someone who was starving."

The newspapers reported on the demonstration and also spoke a lot about Mother Teresa. I knew that she had already opened a house for the homeless in Rome modeled on the one she had in India. My desire to meet her grew even greater, but it seemed difficult, especially since the newspaper I worked for was not interested in an interview with her.

A Friendly Bishop

In 1975 I went to Rome to interview Bishop Pavel Hnilica, a Slovak bishop who had miraculously escaped from the Communist persecution in his country. He was a very unique individual. Although forced to live in exile, he was continuing his apostolic mission to Eastern countries through secret channels.

When I spoke to him, I was aware that he knew Mother Teresa well. In fact, he was the one who had brought her charitable work to the attention of Pope Paul VI and helped her open one of her houses in the Eternal City. After that, the pope had wanted to meet her.

"Would you introduce me to Mother Teresa?" I asked him. From our first meeting, the Slovak bishop had asked me to use the familiar "*tu*" when speaking with him and to call him simply "Fr. Paolo" (the Italian name for "Pavel"). He dressed like a regular priest and hardly ever wore the insignia of a bishop. His home was always full of needy people: refugees from Iron Curtain countries or vagrants. He would meet them in the street where they were begging for food, and rather than giving them his loose change, the bishop would stop to talk to them, asking about their situations and their families. He often brought them home to feed them or to give them lodging while they looked for work and housing. He was a "type" of Mother Teresa himself.

"Would you introduce me to Mother Teresa?" I asked again.

"Of course," said Bishop Hnilica in a joyful voice. "If you write some articles on her and her work, that could be useful. She has already opened two houses for the poor here in Rome, but there are other needs. When Mother Teresa comes to Rome again, I will call you and set up a meeting."

Bishop Hnilica was a powerhouse of initiatives. His mind never stopped. He thought and acted with the typical directness of people who wholeheartedly believe in God. In his mind, all things were possible as long as their purpose was for doing good.

At that time he had a secretarial assistant named Fr. Sergio Mercanzin, a bright young priest from Venice. Bishop Hnilica put me in touch with him, and I asked him to keep reminding the bishop of my desire. I told him I had wanted to meet Mother Teresa for a very long time and explained that I did not want to have a "forced" meeting with her. I did not want to be introduced and then put her on the spot by asking questions that she would feel obliged to answer. I was not interested in that kind of interview. I wanted to have a leisurely conversation with her, to win her trust, to get insights about her life and her extraordinary work, and to understand the feelings and emotions she experienced while living a life among the outcasts of humanity. In brief, I wanted to look into the heart and soul of this woman, who was a saint in my eyes. It was an impertinent desire—perhaps even a bit sacrilegious—but it was what I wanted to do.

Every time I went to Rome, I contacted Bishop Hnilica to see if he had any news about my interview. He would tell me that he had talked to Mother Teresa but had not received a definitive response. She would always reply that she had so many duties that it left her no time to meet with a journalist. She would add that she also did not want people talking about her. Being a polite person, she would say that perhaps the interview could happen at another time when she would be in Rome with fewer pressing affairs.

Finally, one day Bishop Hnilica called me to say that he had set up an appointment for me with Mother Teresa. That was in 1986. Fifteen years had gone by since I was first interested in meeting her, and ten years had gone by since my first request for an interview.

Chapter Four

•

The First Meeting

A journalist meets many people over time—ordinary people, artists, politicians, business owners, military personnel, thieves, murderers, and even saints. Each encounter can be a fascinating and engaging experience for me, especially when in some cases I need to get to know the person, win his or her confidence, and establish a rapport in a very short space of time. If that person is "special," as Mother Teresa was, the experience is unforgettable.

Strolling under Large Trees

The call from Bishop Hnilica saying he had set up an appointment for me with Mother Teresa took me by surprise, especially since it was set for the very next day. I immediately accepted. I had waited for ten years for this meeting, and I was absolutely determined not to miss my chance.

I left Milan that same afternoon for Rome so that I could be ready the next morning. The meeting was for 9:00 a.m., but Bishop Hnilica said that Mother Teresa was in the suburbs of the city, so it would take an hour by car to arrive there.

I went to Hotel Cicerone, where I usually stayed when I was in Rome. It is a very comfortable hotel where I had been staying for years, and I am treated very well there. That night I could not sleep. I kept turning on the light to check the time on my watch. I was very nervous. In the morning, accompanied by Bishop Hnilica and his assistant, Fr. Sergio Mercanzin, I went to Casalina, a suburb of Rome where one of the houses for Mother Teresa's sisters is located.

Mother Teresa was waiting outside, strolling under large trees. There was no garden or beautiful park area that is usually found around convents and religious institutions. The yard looked like a field, a green field that was allowed to grow naturally because the homeowners—in this case, the sisters—had much more important things to do.

Nothing to Tell about Herself

I approached Mother Teresa with a bit of intimidation. Stretching out her hand warmly to me, she said the bishop had told her a lot about me. She looked me over with her inquisitive eyes and smiled at me with a peaceful, relaxed face. I do not believe I was able to think of any response to what she was saying. Perhaps she noticed, so although she was a woman of few words, she continued speaking to me, the bishop, and Fr. Mercanzin. Then she led us to a rough wooden table and benches under a large tree and said, "We can sit here."

After we sat down, I froze up and could not tap into my usual spontaneity. Knowing that I wanted to interview her, she helped me, launching immediately into conversation.

"What would you like me to tell you?" she asked. Her question lingered in the clear morning air. It was just after 9:00, and on certain spring days in the Roman suburbs, the light at that time of day is enchanting.

"I would like you to tell me about yourself and about your wonderful adventure with the poorest of the poor of the world," I replied.

I was immediately aware of the stupidity of my statement. The phrase "wonderful adventure with the poorest of the poor of the world" made me blush. Mother Teresa had certainly noted the generic nature of the phrase and also saw my embarrassment. I noticed the way she was looking at me. She must have understood my discomfort because she became very gentle and almost affectionate. Later, Bishop Hnilica and Fr. Sergio, who both knew her well, mentioned that to me.

"There is nothing to tell about myself. I am a poor sister like so many others," she said. "The Lord gave me a mission, and I am trying to fulfill it as best I can. But he is the author of everything. Jesus loves the poor. They are his favorite children. When he came into this world, he himself was born into a poor family, and the most beautiful words of the gospel are reserved for the poor. We need to talk about them, not about me. I count for nothing."

From Discomfort to Comfort

She spoke with simplicity, but in every word there was some kind of emotional mystery. Every sentence penetrated my heart with strange power. Her tone was subdued and intimate; her voice was persuasive.

As she sat there in front of me, Mother Teresa seemed very small. She was smaller than I had imagined from looking at photographs of her. And she was very thin. Her shoulders were hunched over. She was seated, but she seemed curled up into her seat. In order to look at me, she had to raise her head, and she did it with effort because her shoulders, visibly rigid with arthritis, were forcing her chin to her chest. Lifting her head perhaps caused her pain, but none of us could know for sure.

When she looked at me, I saw clear eyes that had the brightness one sees in children's eyes. However, her hands were gnarled, twisted, worn out by work. Her feet, in rough, heavy sandals, seemed deformed by the thousands of miles she had walked in the rain, in the mud, and over rocks. For more than forty years, Mother Teresa had been in constant motion to bring assistance to those who were suffering. Rain or shine, she always went around on foot, smiling and praying. Her feet had become deformed by that enormous labor.

I had written out a long list of questions. I put the tape recorder on the table in front of her and began to read the first ones. However, I continued to feel uncomfortable. It was Mother Teresa, with her compassion and understanding, who came to my aid, recounting events and amusing anecdotes. However, they had nothing to do with my written questions. Little by little, I was put at ease, and the conversation began to flow.

We stayed under that tree for about two hours. Mother Teresa had said a lot, but I did not succeed in receiving answers to my questions. At a certain point, she got up and said, "I need to leave you now. I have people waiting for me at the house." Turning to me and smiling, she added, "Let's continue this tomorrow if you still want to talk to me."

"Of course I would like to talk to you again," I said. "Thank you so much for your availability. I know you have many pressing duties, so I am grateful that you can give me some of your time. Shall we meet here again tomorrow?"

"No," she said. "Tomorrow let's meet at the church of St. Polycarp outside Rome, where fourteen young sisters of my community will be making their vows. I will be there, and I would very much like you to come. The ceremony will help you understand the spirit of our consecrated life. We will talk after the ceremony. Don't forget. I will be expecting you."

"I will most certainly be there," I said.

Chapter Five

•

TESTIMONY OF LOVE

At precisely 11:00 the next morning, I was at the church of St. Polycarp in Rome. The church was already full of people. Everyone was staring at the main entrance because they wanted to see Mother Teresa. When she made her entrance in the middle of the group of young sisters who were going to make their vows, people began to applaud. Many people were weeping.

Without lifting her gaze, Mother Teresa continued walking in the middle of the group. She walked through the church up to the altar and knelt in a corner.

Equipped with the Greatest Love

The ceremony was very long and truly evocative. The young sisters making their vows had radiant and compassionate faces. Emotion was also seen on the faces of the many sisters who had accompanied them and were sitting in the pews mingled in with the people throughout the church. Some people's eyes were swollen from weeping. As I looked around, I counted about fifty sisters, all dressed in white cotton saris with blue stripes, just like Mother Teresa.

At that time the Missionaries of Charity had four houses in Rome and was engaged in backbreaking ministry. The sisters in front of us, looking so fragile and defenseless, were the ones taking care of the poverty-stricken and abandoned people in the capital of Italy who had been neglected by all the other religious organizations and humanitarian groups.

At night they try to bring a word of comfort and hope in the area of the Termini Train Station, an area filled with people experiencing the most severe hopelessness: people on drugs, prostitutes, the homeless, and thieves. Even the police are hesitant to patrol the area at night, but Mother Teresa's "Indian nuns," equipped with the greatest love, go there. I looked around the church and paid close attention to the sisters kneeling in the pews. Thinking of the very hard life they had embraced, I experienced a feeling of admiration along with some consternation.

They were all young, and some of them were very young. Their faces revealed the concern of those who are always dealing with problems. Their cracked, rough hands spoke of the physical labor of their intensive work. The skin of their faces, lacking any cosmetics or beauty treatments, was nondescript and unimpressive. Their eyes, however, were striking. They had a light that was almost feverish; a strange and powerful energy came forth from them that commanded respect and almost fear.

At the end of the long ceremony, Mother Teresa gave a short speech in English that was translated by another sister. Among other things, she said, "Our work consists in a difficult task. We are accessible to the poor and abandoned twenty-four hours a day. We refuse help to no one. The young people who asked to join this congregation understand the difficulties they will encounter, but they will face them with generosity because their souls are full of love."

Living in Constant Union with God

When Mother Teresa left the church, I went to greet her. She was happy to see me and saw that I had come to meet her as she had asked. Because she had so many things to do that day and would not quite have enough time to talk to me, she asked me to join her in the car that was taking her to the motherhouse at San Gregorio al Celio (St. Gregory on the Caelian Hill) near the Colosseum so that I could ask her questions as we rode. We continued the conversation that we had started the day before.

"The ceremony was very evocative and moving," I said to initiate our conversation.

"Oh, yes, very moving," she said. "I really wanted you to be there. Words alone are insufficient to help people understand certain spiritual realities."

"Before making their vows, what preparation or training do they receive?" I asked.

"When a young girl enters our order, she observes our way of life and the activities we are involved in for a period of time so that she can determine if she truly wants to have that kind of life. Once she makes the decision to join, she is then ready to begin the novitiate, which lasts for two years. During that time, the young woman learns about the work that she will do by actually doing it together with other sisters who have already professed their vows. She will, for instance, assist the dying, help the poor, and beg for food for those who have none. She will perform all the tasks that we are usually involved in, going through this practical test to see if this is the life she wants to choose.

"If she stays on, she professes her vows at the end of two years and commits before God and the Church to seek holiness according to the Rule of our community."

"What does a normal day look like for your sisters?"

"The day consists primarily in prayer. Contrary to appearances, we are not sisters of the 'active life.' We are contemplatives who live in the midst of the world. Prayer, therefore, is fundamental for us. We are always praying: in the streets, during work, and so forth. If we were not in constant union with God, it would be impossible for us to endure the sacrifices that are required to live among the destitute."

"What time do the sisters get up in the morning?"

"At 4:30 a.m. We pray together for an hour and a half. We have breakfast and then go to work from there. The specific duties of the sisters are dictated by the needs in the places where they are working. Here in Rome, for example, my sisters help those who are sick and alone. They help the elderly who cannot take care of themselves. They clean their houses, do the laundry, and act as companions. Often they also beg so that they can buy food for those who have none."

"What time do they go to bed at night?"

"Usually at 10:00 p.m., but if necessary, we work through the night."

"Is this schedule the same for all the houses, or is it adjusted depending on the location in which the sisters work?"

"It is the same for all the houses, but it is not inflexible. The rules are meant to serve the goal, which is doing good for the people we assist. Charity is the rule above all, even if charity needs to be governed by rigorous discipline."

"Do you follow this schedule too?"

"Yes, I am a sister just like the others."

"Don't you find it tiring at your age to get up at 4:30?"

"It is tiring even for the youngest sisters to get up then. But that sacrifice is a way of showing love to Jesus, and my heart is young."

"You have been very sick recently and had heart surgery."

"I am in God's hands. I work for him. I don't have to ask myself if I am well or not. He will tell me himself when it is time to stop."

Sent Out into All the World

"How many sisters belong to your order right now [in 1986]?"

"There are around 3,000 who live in 303 houses scattered across 75 countries. We have requests for 140 new houses, but we cannot satisfy everyone. It would require many more vocations than the ones that the Lord has already given us."

I was curious about Communist countries. "When there were still strict dictatorships in Communist countries that were clearly atheistic and hostile to religion, you were able to obtain permission to open your houses even in those countries. How did things work out in those places?"

"The works of love are the works of peace. We never were interested in politics, and everyone accepted us. The Missionaries of Charity started working in different Communist countries like Poland, Yugoslavia, East Germany, and the Soviet Union before the Iron Curtain fell. We went to those countries because there were poor people there who also needed our love."

"You are Catholic nuns. You help the poor, but you also spread the Catholic faith, right?"

"If someone has a treasure, it is only right to try to share it. However, we never take the initiative to proselytize. Our faith commitment is put into practice by 'demonstration.' We love everyone in concrete ways with the love of God. Our works reveal to the poor and the suffering the love that God has for them.

"The results are always wonderful. One day in India, an American reporter who observed me giving medication to a sick person with gangrene said, 'I wouldn't do that even for a million dollars.' I replied that I would not do it for that amount of money either. 'Rather, I do it for the love of God. This suffering person represents the body of Christ to me.' The reporter was struck by my answer and understood the power that sustains our ministry."

Reflecting the Love of God

She went on to say: "I can give you another example that occurred here in Rome. As they were looking for abandoned people, the sisters came across an old man who was an atheist. His suffering and solitude had made him bitter. He was closed in on himself and would not even say a word to the sisters who had found him. They did not lose heart. They did his laundry, cleaned his house, and even stocked up on food for him. The man, however, continued to not speak. The sisters then decided to visit him twice a day. Finally, after a week, the man was won over by so much care and broke his silence. 'Sisters, you have brought God into my life. Please find me a priest now because I would like to go to confession. I haven't gone for sixty years.'

"The love of the sisters had made this man reflect and facilitated his conversion. They had not spoken to him about God, but he had understood that their behavior could not have been inspired by anyone else."

She shared another example: "In Melbourne, Australia, the sisters came across an alcoholic. He had been in that condition for several years and had lost all his dignity. He was living like an animal. The sisters took him into our House of Mercy, bathed him, clothed him, and began to help him detoxify. After a few weeks, the man was restored and was able to return home. He went to work again. When he cashed his first paycheck, he brought the money to us, saying, 'I want you to be the love of God for others too, just as you were to me.'"

She concluded: "These are a few examples that show it is not necessary to speak about God to convert people. It is enough to demonstrate love."

"What are the principal areas of your ministry?"

"We try to be present wherever there is suffering without hope, that is, wherever the poor and the sick have been completely abandoned. We never made a plan for our activities. We have developed them gradually as needs presented themselves. It has always been God who shows us what we should do."

She went on to explain: "At first, I began by educating the young children of the poor in the slums of Calcutta. Then, I organized some dispensaries to distribute medicine to the sick and food to the hungry. I organized vocational schools to teach the poor how to make a living. And then bit by bit, we took on other ventures in order to be present wherever suffering calls for our help. "

The car we were in turned left, passing by the Colosseum, and drove up a small street toward the very beautiful church of

St. Gregory on the Caelian Hill where the motherhouse of the Missionaries of Charity in Italy is currently located. A variety of people were already waiting for Mother Teresa.

I got out of the car and said good-bye.

"Come back tomorrow morning," she said. "This time I will wait for you at our house here. Mass is at 5:00 a.m. You can come in by that small portico over there to the left of the church. The door will be open."

"I will definitely see you then," I said.

I returned to the Colosseum on foot. A crowd of tourists was swirling around that famous Roman monument. The noonday sun burned my white skin—the skin of a man who normally lives indoors.

Chapter Six

THE MOTHERHOUSE IN ROME

After dinner that night, I said to the desk clerk at the hotel, "Please wake me tomorrow at 4:00 a.m."

"Do you need to catch a plane?" he asked.

"No, I need to meet someone," I replied.

The clerk looked at me, surprised. I had been staying at that hotel for years, so he knew me well and knew that I liked to get up early in the morning to walk though the city. However, I had never gotten up at 4:00 a.m. and certainly never to meet someone.

I slept little that night. I kept thinking of my two meetings with Mother Teresa and of all the things she had told me. I had already begun organizing the material, but I kept thinking all night about her unusual comments that were so far from "normal life" and "normal thinking."

At the wake-up call, I jumped out of bed full of energy. After half an hour, I was in the lobby waiting for a taxi.

The Small Portico on the Side of the Church

At 4:00 a.m. Rome has a particular attraction. The streets are deserted; the palaces and monuments, wrapped in the mysterious shadows that precede dawn, seem to be alive and holding their breath, expecting something extraordinary.

The taxi drove along unhindered. A few windows were lit. A stray dog crossed the street. I was in an expectant mood. I told the taxi driver to drop me off near the Colosseum and climbed up toward San Gregorio al Celio on foot.

The door of the portico on the side of the church that Mother Teresa had pointed out was open. As I entered, the light coming through some windows indicated to me that the chapel was in that area. As I approached, I looked through the windows. Some sisters were already there, kneeling. I took a seat in a corner at the back so as to not disturb them.

The sisters continued to enter, coming from the rooms where they had rested during the night. Mother Teresa also came in and knelt, just like the others, on the bare floor. There was no distinction between her and the other sisters. There was no special place for her—the founder and mother superior of her community.

In all religious communities, the mother superior is revered, served, and treated with deference. But Mother Teresa of Calcutta had not wanted any privileges. She always wanted to be considered on par with the other sisters, even with the newest sisters who had just arrived and were only aspirants or novices. Even in the chapel there that morning, she was mixed in with the other sisters at the back.

I could see her very well from my spot. I watched her attentively throughout the Mass. I knew I should not have been distracted during the service—I should have been praying like the sisters. However, I was sure the Lord would be understanding and sympathetic. When I saw the concentration, the humility, and the tenderness on Mother Teresa's face as she conversed with her God, the very admiration that rose up in me was a prayer.

When the celebrant left the altar at the end of Mass, a sister approached me and signaled me to follow her. She led me to a large room and told me to wait for Mother Teresa, who would arrive soon.

After about ten minutes, Mother Teresa came in carrying a tray with breakfast: coffee, milk, marmalade, bread, and fruit. I felt uneasy because I wanted to stop her from going to any trouble for me, but I did not succeed. She made me sit at the small table in the middle of the room and wanted to serve me. I protested, feeling embarrassed.

Business Cards

Mother Teresa smiled lovingly. She asked me if I preferred honey instead of sugar to sweeten my coffee. Then she explained that she had been delayed in bringing my breakfast because she needed to greet the sisters who were going out into the city to work. "It is a beautiful day and also a bit cool," she said. "They will not suffer from the heat today." She spoke tenderly like a real mother who is concerned about her children.

She asked me if I had liked the ceremony for the profession of vows the day before.

"Yes, very much," I answered.

"You should come visit us in Calcutta," she said. "You could better understand the real spirit of our community and understand the profound significance of the work Jesus has called us to do."

"I would like to visit Calcutta," I said. "I should definitely come. If you give me your address and phone number there, I will write to you and come for a visit."

Mother Teresa took the notebook that I had nearby, which I carry to jot down my thoughts. She opened it to a blank page and wrote her address. Then, smiling, she told me: "One day in America, I met an important person who was very rich. He gave me his business card and asked for mine. 'I don't have one,' I told him. 'What?' he exclaimed, surprised. 'A famous woman like you should have business cards. In America the people who count pay close attention to those. I advise you to get some as soon as possible, and you will see that they are very useful.'

"I listened to that man and had some cards made. But I did not put my title and credentials on them since I do not have any. I am less than nothing. Instead, I wrote a few sentences that represent the principles I live by."

Mother Teresa rummaged through the pockets of her sari and took out one of the cards and gave it to me. It was a dull blue rectangle of poor-quality paper with words in English:

The fruit of SILENCE is Prayer.
The fruit of PRAYER is Faith.
The fruit of FAITH is Love.
The fruit of LOVE is Service.
The fruit of SERVICE is Peace.

On the left side of the card, there were two hands folded in prayer.

"This card," she explained, "allows me to follow the custom of important people whom I often encounter. They give me their card, and I give them mine. That way I can share a good thought, a good message. Who knows if someone reading these lines might not reflect on their importance and significance? I can do some good in this way too."

The Homeless in the Sixteenth-Century Palace

I had never been to the Missionaries of Charity's house in Celio. So far I had met with Mother Teresa outside the city center. I was curious about how the motherhouse that dedicated itself to the poor was maintained.

Mother Teresa accompanied me in my visit to that residence, which was in a very beautiful area. I asked her some questions, but she did not respond. I understood that some of them were not very clear and perhaps not very "Christian." As always, in similar circumstances, she preferred to remain silent. Still very curious, I subsequently asked about the history of the housing complex I was touring with her.

The construction of the complex at San Gregorio where the motherhouse of the Missionaries of Charity is located had its origins in the seventh century. It was built on Celio (the Caelian Hill) halfway between the Colosseum and Circus Maximus. In 1573 it became the property of the Camaldolese Benedictine monks, who used it to offer hospitality to the poor.

After Italy's unification in 1870, the complex was divided in two. One part, comprised of the church and some homes, was kept by the monks. The other part was deemed state property for educational facilities. At first, it housed an institute of pediatric nursing and later, under fascism, a school for social work.

In 1946 the city returned that state property to the Camaldolese monks so that the whole area could continue in its former function as a refuge for the poor. The monks, however, were not able to use it due to the lack of personnel. In 1974 they decided to put the complex at the disposal of Mother Teresa because she would make it a genuine shelter for the poor and abandoned. They informed the city administration of their intended plan and received authorization to proceed.

Ordinance 29527: Notice to Evict

Mother Teresa used the ancient building to set up an extraordinary and efficient residence for the homeless. She set up eighty beds in about twenty rooms. Every night sisters went into the city looking for desperate cases. Unfazed by the evil they would encounter, they went around the subway area under the Termini Station, around the porticos of the Piazza Esedra, around the ruins at the Colosseum—all the areas where victims of despair and misery usually sought refuge. The neediest ones were brought back to the house and cared for with unbounded love.

In a very short time, Mother Teresa's work at San Gregorio became a shining example of Christian charity. Even agnostics and atheists, hearing about the marvelous accomplishments of Mother Teresa, were moved. One famous agnostic polemicist, Augusto Guerriero (known as "Ricciardetto"), wanted to meet Mother Teresa after hearing reports about the undertakings of the sisters in Rome. He found himself deeply moved in her presence, to the point of shedding tears.

However, this dedication of unbounded love toward the poor bothered some people. When the administration of the city of Rome passed into the hands of a Communist majority, the unexpected happened.

On December 31, 1976, the superior of the Camaldolese, who had entrusted San Gregorio al Celio to the Missionaries of Charity, received a registered letter in which the mayor of Rome ordered him to vacate the buildings that housed the sisters and the homeless. The ordinance, listed as "No. 29527," stated:

> We hereby notify you that this administration, because of unavoidable requirements, has an absolute and immediate need for the property in question presently occupied by this religious community. We order you to vacate the building of all persons and equipment within thirty (30) days of receipt of this letter with a notice that noncompliance will result in the initiation of legal action on behalf of the rights and interests of the administration of the city.

It was a real eviction notice. Everything that Mother Teresa and her sisters had accomplished in two years of intense labor was going to have to be interrupted and left behind. There was no consideration either for the heroic spirit of sacrifice demonstrated by the sisters or for the happiness they had brought to so many homeless people.

Serene and unperturbed, the sisters commented, "Jesus has never abandoned us, and he will not abandon us now. He will show us the path to follow and will find us another roof that can protect so many suffering creatures."

However, even though the sisters were resigned to the situation, the general populace most certainly was not. The people of Rome lined up in unity on the side of Mother Teresa. Political and religious authorities intervened, and the mayor had to retract his eviction notice. The sisters remained at San Gregorio and are still there today.

They continued their charitable work, always with the same love and the same self-sacrifice. But that page of Roman history—an eviction notice by the mayor of the Eternal City—will always be history. In a remarkable coincidence, exactly twenty years later, in 1996, another mayor of Rome, the young and forward-looking Francesco Rutelli, made Ordinance 29527 partially recede in people's memories. On May 21 of that year, he proclaimed Mother Teresa an honorary citizen of Italy's capital in an official ceremony in the Julius Caesar Hall at Campidoglio in the presence of many supporters of the city's proclamation.

The Chicken Coop

I learned this entire story only after my visit. While she was showing me around the home that day in 1985, Mother Teresa gave no sign whatsoever of the trial she had endured here years earlier. I was looking at a very beautiful place.

All religious congregations have residential headquarters in Rome. Usually, they are very beautiful large dwellings located in ancient palaces. They generally house the top superiors of an order and function as the operating center for liaison with the Vatican. Religious congregations need to keep up the exterior appearances of these dwellings because they represent the congregations. I immediately assumed that the motherhouse of the Missionaries of Charity in Rome would also have those characteristics. The dwelling was, in fact, very beautiful, situated in an ancient palace of the famous complex of St. Gregory the Great, but that was not the end of the story.

The beautiful sixteenth-century building that had been the head-quarters of the Camaldolese in the past had been turned into a residence for the homeless by the sisters. The poor and homeless that they gathered every night off the streets of Rome were thus treated like royalty in an authentic villa in the most beautiful of all the residences that the Missionaries of Charity have throughout the world.

The sisters—religious of the Roman Catholic Church, spouses of Christ—lived, instead, in the chicken coop. That's right! They had built a little convent by refurbishing the villa's old chicken coop. It was this chicken coop that Mother Teresa wanted as the residential headquarters for the Missionaries of Charity in Rome. Living there in extreme simplicity, they received visitors—famous and powerful figures, bishops, cardinals, businessmen, politicians, and ordinary people—giving everyone a moving example of absolute poverty.

The small convent is neat and clean, but it still has the basic structure of a chicken coop. The rooms are small with gray walls. The roof does not have any insulation, so in the summer the humidity can be oppressive, and in winter it can be freezing. There is no heating equipment of any kind, and one can feel the cold of winter even in Rome. The most genuine poverty governs absolutely, and it is so real and concrete that one could almost reach out and touch it. Walking down a kind of corridor that divides the building in two and realizing that young sisters live here in this shanty-town structure, one might feel a sense of oppression and dismay that not even the sweet, steady smiles on the sisters' faces succeed in dispelling.

"We Missionaries of Charity must suffer with Christ," said Mother Teresa when she saw the disconcerted look on my face. "Only in this way are we able to share the suffering of the poor. Our order could die out if the sisters did not walk in Christ's footsteps, in his suffering, and did not live in poverty.

"Strict poverty is our safeguard. We do not want to start by serving the poor and unwittingly slide into serving the rich, as has happened to other religious congregations in the course of history. To understand and be able to help those who are deprived of everything, we need to live as they do. The radical difference is that those we help are poor by force of circumstances, while we are poor by our free choice, out of love."

Absolute Poverty

Every time Mother Teresa said the word "poverty"—and she always gave it an absolute meaning, which is typical of someone who has nothing—I could not wrap my head around it. I could not fully understand. I knew that all religious communities, especially "mendicant" orders, profess the vow of poverty, but it seemed that things were somehow different for the Missionaries of Charity. I therefore asked Mother Teresa for fuller explanations about the legal guidelines and principles of her community, and she would always say the same things, which still did not quite make sense to me.

Even today I do not believe I fully understand. In my view, it is impossible for an organization like the Missionaries of Charity, in the way Mother Teresa seemed to intend it, to continue to operate in our world without miraculous interventions of Divine Providence.

This is the case precisely because of their vow of poverty. Members of various religious institutes and congregations profess a vow of poverty, but it usually entails a vow that is not absolutely rigid. Even those institutions that were once ruled by rigorous evangelical poverty have today adapted to the practical and functional needs of a society that is administratively very complicated.

Mother Teresa, with her Missionaries of Charity, has instead returned to ancient times and has restored that vow to its ancient unyielding and sublime rigor. It is difficult to imagine how a society of around five thousand people today can govern themselves and operate while keeping such a vow. Every residence of the Missionaries of Charity entails expenditures in order to exist; that is, it needs an influx of capital to draw on at its very beginning and for its continuing operation.

However, the Missionaries of Charity is not engaged in any productive industry. Its activity is essentially charitable, aimed at helping the poorest of the poor. The sisters beg for money to give it to those who have none or to spend it to buy food, clothing, and medicine. It is therefore an activity that is continuously operating at a heavy financial loss. While they spend a lot, there is no fixed and stable income, no safety nets to replace the money that has been spent.

Mother Teresa's army is enormous. The thousands of sisters who operate in more than seven hundred houses scattered among more than one hundred nations today cost a lot of money. Moreover, they are responsible for hundreds of thousands of people: the poor, abandoned children, the dying, the homeless, the handicapped, unwed mothers, those afflicted with AIDS and leprosy. This is an army of infinitely more people that must be housed, fed, clothed, and cared for medically, sometimes with costly surgeries and with medicine that is not easy to acquire. Their operation, in brief, costs a lot of money but is unable to provide for itself.

Small Gestures of Love

The total cost for the entire enterprise, then, involves staggering numbers whose administration could cause anyone to have heart failure. Only a very wealthy person with a lot of capital and enormous revenues from business interests could peacefully take on such an enterprise. I pointed that out to Mother Teresa and asked her how she went about tracking down all the money to keep going.

She smiled and answered, "Providence. Providence takes care of it." It was an easy, evasive answer, so I returned to the point. Then Mother Teresa repeated the specific concepts behind the vow of poverty that she had intended for her community: a total and absolute poverty that involved not only each individual sister but also the community as a whole as a legal entity. In other religious institutions, the vow of poverty is made by the individual. As an entity, the institution can own things, have income, and be, in a certain sense, "rich." This is not the case, however, for the Missionaries of Charity. Even as an entity, the sisters possess nothing: The community does not have income, does not have steady revenues, and does not receive any stipends for the work they do. They live only by charity.

"In addition to the three traditional vows of poverty, chastity, and obedience that are common to all members of the religious of institutions," Mother Teresa said, "we take a fourth vow. We take a specific vow that characterizes us. It is a kind of vow of 'super-poverty': We commit to lovingly and 'freely' serving all the poor. That vow means we cannot accept any recompense for our work."

She admitted: "It is true that a lot of money is needed to keep our order and our activities going. We trust Providence to send it through generous people who want to collaborate with us. We live from offerings, alms, and small gestures of love from thousands of people. In line with trusting Providence, we do not accept any kind of 'fixed' assistance—no loans, no stipends, no subsidies. I do not want people to pledge to give a certain sum of money at regular intervals—every week, every month, or every year. Any fixed income would allow us to plan ahead for programs, activities, and projects, but with that kind of financial underpinning, we would no longer be daughters of Providence."

No Thought for Tomorrow

Using these principles, Mother Teresa has given life to a marvelous and mammoth organization that functions perfectly and offers joy and hope to thousands and thousands of desperate people. It is an amazing miracle of love and faith in God. One would indeed need a rock-solid faith to avoid being completely overwhelmed by anxiety every morning just thinking about how such a massive operation could possibly get through the day without collapsing.

"The essential rationale for this poverty," she explained, "is based in love. The people we help are involuntarily poor; we, on the other hand, become poor as they are through a loving choice. We want to be like Jesus who, although he was rich, chose to be born, to live, and to work among the poor. The constitution of our community says that we will rely completely on Divine Providence. As members of Christ, who lived from alms during his public life and whom we serve in the sick and the poor, we are not ashamed to beg from door to door."

In order to remain faithful to this remarkable ideal of gospel life, Mother Teresa has accustomed her sisters not to think about the next day. She has taught them in the constitution that they must leave their projects for the future to the omnipotent God. Yesterday is gone, tomorrow has not yet come, so there is only today to make Jesus known and to love and serve him.

For each individual sister, the Rule allows for a personal wardrobe of clothing reduced to the bare essentials: a white tunic that covers the sister from her neck to her ankles and wrists with a white sari on top of that and rough sandals for her feet. Every sister has three tunics and two saris. When a sister needs to move to another house, she is ready in ten minutes. Everything she owns can fit into a small bag.

The Rule still requires that the houses where the sisters live should be modest and simple and should resemble the homes of the poor as much as possible. In Third World countries, the sisters often live in actual shacks and squalid shanties. In the spirit of poverty, they also renounce "privacy." Each sister sleeps in a room together with her colleagues, without even a small corner she can call her own.

Chapter Seven

•

THE "CARESSES" OF PROVIDENCE

One day, after Mother Teresa had spoken to me about the absolute poverty she desired for her community, I said to her, "But, then, in order to keep your sisters and your charitable works going, miracles must be necessary."

"That is exactly right," she said, smiling at the astonished expression that she saw on my face. "Daily miracles. Every day God does real miracles for us. We can certify that concretely. If those daily miraculous signs did not happen, we could not go forward; we could not do anything."

A Constant State of Emergency

She looked at me. My astonishment was growing to the point of verging on skepticism. I doubted what she was telling me.

"Are you talking about real, authentic miracles?" I asked.

"Yes, concrete miracles," she replied. "I call them the 'caresses' of Providence, but they are real miracles."

She continued looking at me for a few moments, and then, turning her gaze from me, she said in a strong, decisive voice, "My work was willed by Jesus. He is the one who *needs to* think about how to move it forward."

She emphasized the words "needs to" in such a definitive way that it gave me chills. I had the impression that her statement was not addressed to me as an explanation but to "Someone" whom I was not seeing. It seemed like a challenge. It was an affirmation, but also an insistent prayer.

After a long silent pause, Mother Teresa continued in a gentle, soft voice. "Providence generously takes care of my sisters and the people we help every day. It happens through so many generous people: businessmen, agencies, industries, oil companies, governments. It also happens particularly through the small offerings from people of modest means. These are the offerings that have the greater value because people have to sacrifice for them. Because of that, their almsgiving is an authentic act of love.

"Because of all that we need in our houses to serve the people who ask us for help, we are in a constant state of emergency. None of the sisters responsible for running a house could sleep peacefully unless she had immense faith in God. We almost never have what we need for a week, and sometimes not even what we need to get through the day. However, a solution—and sometimes at the last minute—always arrives. The Lord inspires a variety of donors for a wide variety of reasons to bring us the help that is vital for us. If that help did not arrive, we would find ourselves in deep trouble."

Then she shared some examples. "In Calcutta we cook for nine thousand people every day. One morning a sister told me we had nothing in the pantry. It was Thursday, so it looked like it would be a very difficult weekend. It was the first time I was faced with such an urgent need. 'We need to warn the people,' the sister said. 'No, let's wait,' I told her. 'Go into the chapel and present the whole situation to Jesus.' I prayed too and waited for events to unfold.

"At 9:00 a.m. Friday morning, a truck arrived that was full of bread, marmalade, and milk. The supplies were intended for school meals throughout the city, but that morning the government had decided to close the schools, and all those food provisions were no longer needed. I tried to find out later why the schools had been unexpectedly closed, but I was never given a reason. I believe God intervened to help us. In fact, the poor people were able to eat to their complete satisfaction for two days.

"On another occasion the sisters had no wood for cooking. There was a large pot of curry on the stove. After a while the doorbell rang, and there was a benefactor with a load of wood.

"One afternoon the novice in charge of the kitchen told me that we had no more rice. We did not have even one rupee to go buy any. 'Go into the chapel to pray,' I told her. At 6:30 p.m. a woman we did not know came to the door with a large sack of rice. 'I felt led to bring this to you,' she said. The bag had enough rice for dinner that night."

Medicine from London

Other miracles occurred. "One time a man came looking for me. He was crying because his only son was about to die. The specialist he consulted said he could save the boy only with a special medicine that was very expensive and practically nonexistent in India. He had written down the prescription anyway, and now the man was asking me to help him.

"In my attempt to ease his sorrow, I told him to be calm. 'I will get the medicine from England,' I promised. However, he had hardly left when I realized that I had put myself in a real dilemma. It would not be easy to get that medicine from London, and even if I succeeded, it would take time, and the boy was about to die.

"As I was mulling this over, one of our donors arrived carrying the usual satchel of medicine that he had collected from the homes of rich people. We usually collect medicine that is expired because it is still valuable for our poor people who cannot buy it. As I was checking over what he had brought, I immediately spotted a small bottle. It was precisely the medicine the dying boy needed, and it was the exact dose prescribed by the specialist."

Houses in London and Agra

"I was looking for a house in London with some of the sisters," she said, "so that we could open up a new home. A lady had a house that seemed to fit our requirements perfectly, so we went to see her. After we visited the house, she told us in an abrupt tone, 'It costs 6,500 pounds, and the whole amount is due now.' She added, 'I don't believe in anything, and I don't do charity for anybody.'

"The situation was quite difficult. We did not have any money, but at the same time, we needed that house. We decided to split up and go around the city to visit friends and sympathizers and to ask for their help in an effort to solicit a good portion of the amount. When we reunited at the end of the day, we added up what we had collected. It came to 6,500 pounds exactly.

"One of my sisters called me one day from Agra in India, asking for 50,000 rupees to start an orphanage. 'It is impossible,' I told her. 'Where do you think I can find such an amount?' A few minutes later, the phone rang again. It was the editor of a newspaper telling me, 'The Philippine government has awarded you the Magsaysay Prize and a sum of money.' 'How much?' I asked.

'The amount is 50,000 rupees,' he replied. In that case, I could see that God wanted an orphanage in Agra."

Not Even One Drop of Water

Mother Teresa told me about other kinds of miracles too. "During the rainy season, a steady rain was coming down in Calcutta. I was concerned because I had set up ninety-five crates of powdered milk in the courtyard that would be ruined by the rain. 'What should I do, Lord?' I prayed. 'The milk is outside.' It seemed like Jesus was not hearing me because the heavy rain was nonstop. I grabbed a crucifix and took it into the middle of those crates under the rain to make sure that he was aware of the situation. But that did not work to stop the rain either.

"After five days the sky finally cleared up. The crates were floating in water. We went to open them to see if we could possibly salvage any of the powdered milk, and we saw to our great amazement that all of it was perfectly dry. Some of the crates had damaged tops, but not even one drop of water had penetrated the crates.

"Many people are amazed to hear us tell about events like this, but there is nothing extraordinary here: It is all simple and logical. If I see a poor person, I have a deep desire to help him or her. But I am only one person. How much greater must Jesus' desire be to help us when we have difficulties? He, too, has a heart, and it is a heart that loves immensely. Jesus is in heaven with a body, so he is a person like us, and he is amazing—very kind and very caring. He is never indifferent to our suffering and our concerns.

We need to believe in his love without question in order to be able to witness his miracles every day."

Benefactors

Mother Teresa talked about benefactors. "Often the Lord uses our neighbor to help us. He inspires people to love us, to be sympathetic to us, to want to collaborate. But it is always he who is acting on our behalf.

"One day a young Hindu couple came to me to give an offering for the poor. Since it was a large sum, I asked where they had gotten so much money. 'We were married two days ago,' they replied. 'We had put aside a sum of money for our wedding celebration, and the rest was given to us by friends and relatives. At the last minute, we decided to buy only necessary things and to give the rest to you. We love each other very much and thought it would be good to share our love with the poor people you serve.'

"A while ago in Calcutta, there was a shortage of sugar for a period of time. Throughout the city the word went out that we had no more sugar for our orphans, so many people came to help us. One night a couple came with their six-year-old son. They were holding a jar. For a week the little boy had refused to eat sugar so that he could give it to those less fortunate than himself."

A "Secret Co-Worker"

There was a special kind of benefactor, however. "We have people scattered throughout the world who cooperate with us and are organized into groups that give us valuable help by collecting clothes, bandages, medicine, and all the things that are useful for our dispensaries. The simple and generous sacrifices of thousands of people who are unknown to us enable us to help so many people. However, I rely only on prayer. I never think about money. We want to perform the work of the Lord, and he has to think about the means for us to do that. If he does not send it to us, it means that he does not want us to do this or that activity.

"Because of this, the people I consider the greatest co-workers for myself and the sisters are the sick who offer their suffering to God for us, and the contemplatives—monks and nuns—who pray for our work. Many handicapped people who cannot do any activity are bound to us by an agreement to collaborate. Each of them adopts one sister and offers his or her prayer and suffering for that sister. A very deep bond is established between each of them and a particular sister, and they become like one person.

"I, too, have a 'secret co-worker.' She is a Belgian woman I have known for more than thirty years. Her name is Jacqueline de Decker, and she is very ill. She has undergone seventeen surgeries and endures every pain to help me complete my mission well. Every time I have a special task to complete, she is the one who gives me the necessary strength and courage. In fact, at those times her suffering increases. Sometimes she writes me, 'I am sure you have a lot to do right now—a lot of travel, work, and speeches. I know that because of the pain I feel in my back and because of other suffering that has become especially intense.'

"Jacqueline is never wrong. The mysterious laws that govern people's spirits allow for these exchanges. She is the sick friend who accomplishes on my behalf the most difficult part of my work."

•

Chapter Eight

CONTINUOUS PRAYER

In my various conversations with Mother Teresa, the topic of prayer was constant. She resorted to prayer for every situation, and not just for complicated, difficult situations for which heaven's help was indispensable. She prayed for the smallest, most insignificant things. She explained it was because, for her, prayer did not mean "asking" God for something but "talking with him," "conversing with him," "trusting him" for everything at all times, confident that he would intervene. Prayer for her was "daily bread" or the "oxygen" she needed to live.

Ecstasy in Prayer

One day, with a hint of irony, I asked her, "Are you and your sisters always praying?" Mother Teresa noticed the playful tone of my voice, and she communicated that to me with one of her frequent silent pauses.

"It is true; we are always praying," she said when she continued the conversation. "As I often repeat, we are not sisters of 'the active life.' We are contemplatives who live in the midst of the world. Prayer, therefore, is fundamental for us. Our life should be a continuous prayer. It is prayer, and only prayer, that gives us the strength to face the sacrifices involved in our mission."

On many occasions I observed Mother Teresa while she was engaged in her habit of continuous prayer. Prayer for her was almost a conditioned reflex. When she was with other people, if they began speaking among themselves, she would take the opportunity to bow her head and close her eyes. It is as if she turned to "Someone" who lived within her. All of this happened in a natural, spontaneous manner, and other people did not even notice.

When Mother Teresa prayed in an "official" or formal way—reciting traditional prayers or attending Mass—she seemed to be in ecstasy. She was in profound concentration, and her whole being, including her body, was involved in prayer.

The first time I saw her like that has stayed so vivid in my mind that even to this day, many years later, when I think of Mother Teresa, I see her that way. It was during the Mass at St. Polycarp's in Rome, when the young sisters had professed their vows. She was kneeling in a corner with her hands folded in prayer and her head bent, motionless as a statue. I knew she had arthritis, so it had to be very painful to keep that position for any length of time, but her composure revealed her deep conviction of being in God's presence.

Real Conversation with God

One time we were at her house in Rome. Bishop Hnilica had accompanied me, as he often did, and his driver had brought us there. That day we had all spoken together for a long time. At a certain point, Mother Teresa remembered that she had a commitment and asked what time it was.

"It's 11:00 a.m.," I said after checking my watch.

"I need to go to the Vatican. I am late," she said, getting up. Bishop Hnilica offered to drive her.

"Thank you. That would be a big favor," she said, looking concerned. "I can't keep the pope waiting," she added, smiling. I sat in the back of the car next to her; the bishop sat in front next to the driver. "My driver is very skilled," he said. "He knows all the tricks for dealing with the chaotic traffic in Rome. You'll see. He will make up for lost time, and we will definitely arrive at the Vatican on time."

The car drove off very quickly. Mother Teresa was looking out the window. Her face was serene. After a few minutes, she asked us to pray with her. She made the sign of the cross and took a rosary out of a pocket in her sari and began to pray. She prayed slowly in a subdued voice, saying the Our Father and the Hail Mary in Latin. We prayed along with her.

The car sped along through heavy traffic. At times it would stop abruptly, swerving around other cars. Then it would quickly speed off again, approaching curves fearlessly and just missing other impatient and aggressive drivers, whose horns were relentless. I was clutching the door handle and looking at our very bold and daring driver with concern, but Mother Teresa was absorbed in prayer and did not notice anything else.

Curled up on the seat, she was in conversation with God. Her eyes were closed. Her wrinkled face, bent down to her chest, was transfigured. She almost seemed to be emitting light.

The words of her prayer were precise, clear, and slow, almost as if she were pausing to savor the significance of each word. Her prayer did not have the rhythm of a repetitious formula but the freshness of dialogue, of a lively and passionate conversation. It seemed that Mother Teresa was truly speaking to an invisible presence.

When we finished the rosary, Bishop Hnilica started talking to me, pointing out the Roman monuments that we were passing along the street. I was listening, but I was actually concentrating on watching Mother Teresa, who continued to be absorbed in a silent conversation with God.

She still had her eyes closed and her head bent. Her lips were moving slightly. Only when we were about to arrive at St. Peter's Square, after an hour of driving, did she turn to us and engage in conversation with her usual courtesy.

We stopped at the entrance to the Vatican where the Swiss guards were posted and got out of the car. Bishop Hnilica told us to wait as he went to make a call. Some young girls recognized Mother Teresa and ran up to her, shouting, "Mother Teresa! Mother Teresa!" They were kissing her hands and asking for her autograph. Mother Teresa greeted them and then humbly and quietly moved off to the side. Again I saw her lips moving in a whisper, just as I had seen when she was sitting next to me in the car. She was still praying.

Prayers Always Granted

One day, out of the blue, she asked me if I went to church from time to time.

"Of course," I replied. "I go to Mass every Sunday with my family."

"I don't mean Sunday Mass," she said. "Do you ever go to church during the day to find Jesus?"

Her question took me aback completely. I confessed that I never did that. I said I never really thought about it. She smiled at me.

"You should do it," she said. "Jesus is there waiting for you. He is 'really' there. Like the *Catechism* explains, his presence is 'truly, really, and substantially' there [1374]. It means that he is there in body, soul, and divinity—that is the way he was present to the apostles in Jerusalem and when he appeared to the apostles after his resurrection.

"The presence of Jesus in the Eucharist is a very wonderful and beautiful mystery. You should go often to find Jesus—at least every time you go by a church. It is not necessary to stop for a long time or to say a lot of prayers. No. You need to make yourself seen and just sit for a little bit in front of him and remain there. You do not need to say anything. You need to listen. He will be the One to talk, and that is the best prayer. Traditional prayers can help because our minds are so easily distracted. But if someone learns to listen, to listen attentively with the heart, then he or she will find a fountain of miraculous strength and can face any sacrifice, any difficulty. That person will feel 'embraced' by Jesus."

I asked her: "In the gospel, one day the disciples say to Jesus, 'Teach us to pray,' and after having presented the beautiful prayer of the Our Father, Jesus continues to exhort his disciples to have faith and trust in God and insists, 'Ask, and it will be given to you; seek, and you will find; knock, and it will be opened to you' [Luke 11:9]. However, in practice only a few people ask and always obtain answers. Why is that?"

She replied, "Prayer is always heard and granted by God. That is an absolute certainty. Jesus himself said that in what you just quoted. Let us not forget that Jesus revealed to us that God is 'Father.' A father wants good and not evil for his children—the good, however, seen from the perspective of absolute and total reality. Therefore, if we ask, it is because we think that what we ask for is going to be something good for us. But God sees the future, he sees what is truly good for us, and he answers us only if what we ask for is really fruitful for us. Otherwise, he does not answer us, in the sense that he does not give us what we ask for because it would be harmful for us. Instead, he gives us something better than what we asked for.

"He is like a mother who picks up her baby who is asking for a dangerous toy. She clasps him closely to herself and kisses him to show that she loves him, even though she is not granting his request because it would be bad for him. I have seen so many mothers crying and praying desperately for their small children who are afflicted with incurable diseases. Their prayers are almost always without respite night and day. That comes from thinking that Jesus is absent."

In a pained voice, she continued: "No, no, no. They should not think that. I am certain that faced with the suffering of these mothers, Jesus himself has a heart full of suffering. But he knows that suffering is important. It is part of his passion on the cross that saved all of humanity. We would need to have a long conversation on the meaning of suffering and on the mystery of sorrow, but I can assure you that Jesus always, always answers prayers."

The "Dark Night of the Soul"

She was speaking with passion. One could see that she was truly in love with Jesus. I assumed, therefore, that she would have had real encounters with him and would have seen him from time to time—or other things similar to what we read about in the biographies of the saints.

However, that was not the case. We now have letters she wrote to her confessor and pages from her diaries that were published after her death. From those writings it is clear that Mother Teresa had lived in a terrible state of "spiritual dryness" for years and years—an ordeal of doubts, uncertainties, and darkness. She would be smiling, but inside she felt dead. It was an actual and terrible "dark night of the soul," as the mystics call it. Even though she was talking to me about Jesus in such a passionate way, her heart was as dry as a desert. But her will was like granite in wanting to believe in Jesus and to believe in that kind of suffering that leads to purified love.

A sister who often accompanied Mother Teresa on trips recounted some very telling incidents to me. "Mother Teresa was always thinking about Jesus," she said to me. "She took advantage of every opportunity, no matter how small, to demonstrate her love to him, to tell him that she loved him. She would constantly repeat, 'Everything for Jesus.' Every little suffering and every setback, humiliation, or defeat were for her an occasion to tell Jesus about her love. She did not complain or lose patience or let herself be discouraged. She would just repeat, 'Everything for Jesus.'

"Sometimes she would make small gestures that could even seem infantile. But for people who are in love, nothing is infantile; everything becomes an occasion to demonstrate love to the beloved. For example, I had observed at meals that when fruit was served, Mother Teresa always took an orange. One day I told her that a banana might do her more good because it had more nutrients and calories. She stated that it was true that a banana was more nutritious, but since an orange was made up of several sections, it allowed her to demonstrate her love better to Jesus. Eating each section, she would repeat, 'Jesus, I love you.'

"Up until 1982 she signed the letters she sent to sisters with 'Mother.' After 1982, however, she started signing them with 'Mother Teresa, MC' [the abbreviation for "Missionaries of Charity"]. At that time she was suffering from crippling arthritis in her hands that caused her intense pain, so much so that it was necessary to make a special pen for her that she could hold in her fingers. She was asked why she had changed the way she signed her letters and had chosen a much longer name than simply 'Mother,' which made it more painful because of her arthritis. She replied, 'The word "Mother" consists of a few letters, and to write it I suffer and struggle little. However, "Mother Teresa, MC" is a signature with many more letters and is more painful for me, so I can tell Jesus with those many more letters that I love him.'"

It was only after her death—when it became known that she had experienced the "dark night of the soul" for years—that those small details took on greater significance. Like so many of the things she did, it was a way of deliberately reasserting tens of times every day a faith in God that she was no longer feeling and a love for Jesus inside her that seemed lifeless. Her tenacious, determined, rock-solid will had allowed her to journey toward God, even if around her there was the pitch-black darkness of the crushing "night of the soul." This was a martyrdom that shows how gigantic her love was.

•

Chapter Nine

A Mother's Heart

There are mountains of photographs of Mother Teresa. Although she was a shy and retiring person, she was one of the most beloved people of her generation. Her popularity was so great that whenever she took part in a public event, all the cameras were aimed in her direction. Newspapers, magazines, and television channels frequently sent their correspondents to Calcutta to do stories on her. She never avoided those requests because she knew that her picture would call the world's attention to the problems to which she had dedicated her life.

Dying from Lack of Love

Dramatic photographs have often been published of Mother Teresa as she went around Calcutta among the poor, the lepers, the homeless in dilapidated huts in slums, and the dying. In these photos, Mother Teresa seems sad and concerned, her face marked by wrinkles and burdened with weariness. On the other hand, in the photos in which she is shown with children, she seems like another person. Her face is peaceful and relaxed, and her eyes are shining. One can see that she is filled with great love and a compassionate maternal feeling.

However, even when she is holding a baby in her arms, Mother Teresa is rarely smiling. This is because the babies were abandoned, orphaned, or sick; some were even survivors of massacres, their eyes full of terrifying images. Holding them to her breast, she was trying to make them experience genuine affection in an attempt to alleviate their sorrow and fear, but perhaps without succeeding in forgetting, even at that moment, the sad and unjust situation in which those small innocent ones were found.

"Babies," she said, "are the most beautiful gifts that God can give, but people in their selfishness do not always appreciate them. Often the babies are rejected, abandoned, and even killed. I have always fought against these crimes. I do everything I can to bring attention to this problem.

"Babies have always been a very important part of my life and work. When I started with my new mission in 1948, I began with five abandoned babies. They were living in a shack on the outskirts of Calcutta in the most wretched part of the city. I had nothing, but I went to gather food out of the garbage for them. We were together. I loved them, and they were happy. There is no greater sadness in the world than the sadness due to lack of love. I have seen babies let themselves die because no one loved them."

Rescued from the Streets

The plight of abandoned babies is among the most incomprehensible of all situations. Rarely does an animal abandon its offspring. Human beings, however, do. This is a crime that occurs in rich countries as well as poor ones. This happened in the past when people were considered less civilized, but it continues to happen in our day as well.

Some religious institutes are known for caring for children in a variety of ways. Many religious communities of sisters have even been founded with the express purpose of caring for orphans and children abandoned by their parents. The Missionaries of Charity, in the multiplicity of its charitable works, also assists abandoned children.

In India the problem of abandoned children is greater than in other countries. The extreme poverty that affects a large part of the population breaks up nuclear families. The spread of disease can result in the birth of handicapped children, who are then rejected. A widespread prejudice leads to the neglect of and disinterest in female newborns. It is very easy, therefore, to find newborns babies in India abandoned in churches or simply thrown away in the garbage. In Calcutta this was particularly the case when Mother Teresa began her mission to the poorest of the poor in 1948 because the city was going through one of the most difficult times in its history.

Mother Teresa founded the first home for those babies in 1954. She called it "Shishu Bhavan," which means "Home for Children." Police and citizens quickly began to bring children there from all over the city, and the home soon became too small for all of its residents. She had to open another Shishu Bhavan and then more of them.

"I am mother to thousands of abandoned babies," she told me. "I took them in from sidewalks, from garbage dumps, from sewers. The police brought some, and so did hospitals where children had been rejected by their mothers. I rescued them, saw them grow, and made them study."

The Children Who Stay

Different things happened for those children. "For many I found a family who would adopt them, and they are doing well. They are all over the world—America, India, and Europe. They have gotten jobs, and some of them have become important people.

"They always remember me. The adopting parents have continued sending me photographs to let me see how the children are growing. I receive photos of them dressed up like cowboys with toy guns; on sleds in the snow in Switzerland; on horseback in England; at school with their friends; at the university when they are receiving their diplomas; at their place of work. I keep a large album in Calcutta with their pictures. When I look at it, I always experience great joy because I feel that I loved these children as a real mother would, the way that Jesus taught me.

"There were a lot of adoptions in India too, but that country has special problems. By tradition young couples are supposed to submit to the husband's parents; the parents are the ones in charge. When the daughter-in-law does not succeed in producing a grandson, there is trouble. That is especially true of rich families. The parents tell their sons, 'We have land, houses, jewelry, but you do not have children to whom we can leave our riches.' They urge their sons to abandon their wives and to marry other women so that they can have grandsons.

"However, I have increasingly found young newlyweds who are able to reject these traditions. The husbands do not want to abandon the wives they love, so they try to find a solution for being childless precisely through the generous and enlightened choice of adoption.

"Some people do not have the courage to stand up to their parents, but they come to me too and ask for help. To help in that kind of situation, sometimes we have had recourse to indirect means. These young husbands tell their parents that their wives are pregnant. Then they go on a long vacation, at the end of which they are supposed to go directly to the clinic where we have found an abandoned newborn for them. They go home with the baby as though it were theirs, and everyone is happy. This approach has saved the unity of many families, some of whom are rich and powerful. Some of those babies now have very important positions in society.

"Unfortunately, I do not succeed in having all my children adopted. Some of them stay with me. They tend to be the handicapped, the mentally challenged, and invalids. Nature was cruel to them, but they are children of God and have a great need for love. They are my favorite children."

A New Scourge

Mother Teresa also spoke of desperate cases concerning children. "One time in India, I was asked to take an eight-month-old who had been abandoned along with five of his brothers. The father had left the family, and they were trying to survive before the baby's birth. The mother died of hardship and privation. The baby and his brothers were dying of hunger.

"Even though he was so young, the baby was already numb because of his suffering. In fact, he could not even cry. Lying on his pallet, filthy and covered with lice, he kept his eyes fixed on the ceiling. Only after months of effective treatment and care did he recover his voice and begin to cry.

"Many of the babies I take in die after a few days. They die because they are too small. Mothers cause them to be born prematurely so that they can be free of them. Some weigh less than two pounds and do not even know how to suck.

"We try to rescue them by nourishing them through their nostrils, or we try to give them strength with a drip feed. They struggle desperately to live, but they often cannot. Sometimes they have been poisoned. In fact, some mothers, wanting to be free of their babies before the time of birth, drug themselves and thus poison their babies that way.

"At times some hospitals tell us that it is useless to take in such tiny babies because it is clear that they cannot survive, but we take them anyway. We want them to feel the warmth of love in the few hours they still have in this world and to be able to close their eyes in the arms of someone who loves them.

"Every human being suffers when he or she is not loved, and a baby—even the tiniest one—experiences that and suffers more than any other person. To refuse love to such tiny people is like collaborating in killing them.

"These days a scourge has come upon humanity: AIDS. Someone has called it 'the plague of the twentieth century.' It is worse than leprosy. It is hard to find people who are willing to care for those infected with AIDS. These poor people are abandoned by their very own family members. But they, too, are children of God and need love. Because of our love for Jesus, we dedicate ourselves to them as well. We have already opened up some homes to care for AIDS patients in several nations.

"One special problem occurs for the children of those who have AIDS. The babies are born already infected, and they are immediately surrounded with suspicion and fear. They are viewed with horror and almost with hate. The lack of love makes them suffer terribly.

"We want to help them because these babies are innocent creatures. Their lives will be full of misery because of this disease. We need to do whatever we can to alleviate their suffering. We want to help them know that God loves them and that precisely because of their suffering they are especially loved by the heavenly Father."

A "Spiritual" Godmother

Aware of Mother Teresa's great love for children, I asked her for big favors on some occasions. I thought she would say no, but because it involved babies, she did whatever she could to accommodate me.

I am very good friends with the singer Al Bano. The friendship arose at the beginning of his career and has been ongoing. In fact, I was one of the witnesses at his wedding, and he is the godfather of one of my children.

On Christmas Day in 1985, he became a father for the third time—to a wonderful little girl called Cristel. It was at a time when he had a large number of commitments, so he could not find a time to arrange her baptism. He wanted to hold a large party in his home area of Cellino San Marco in southeast Italy. He was hoping to have the baptism in a small church that he had built on his property. However, being very religious, he was concerned that the sacred Rite of Baptism would turn into a worldly celebration with photographers, reporters, and television cameras, as had happened at his wedding ceremony and, to some extent, at the baptisms of his first two children.

While he delayed in order to organize a ceremony that would be appropriate, time passed. One day in May of 1986, Bano shared his concern with me and asked me to help him plan the ceremony for Cristel's baptism, but not at Cellino San Marco.

"I want a wonderful religious celebration that is protected from public curiosity," he said, "so please do not say anything to anybody. I understand that the public wants to know and wants to see it. I will accommodate them by assigning one photographer to take pictures that can then be distributed to all the newspapers."

"I will see what I can do," I told him.

I knew that Bano and his wife, Romina Power, had great admiration for Mother Teresa, so I thought about arranging Cristel's baptism in Rome and asking Mother Teresa to be godmother to the little girl. It seemed like an impossible dream, given Mother Teresa's numerous commitments, but she had gotten me accustomed to surprises, so I decided to try.

I talked about it with Bishop Hnilica, who seemed in favor of it, so he asked Mother Teresa. She responded that as a sister of the Missionaries of Charities, she could not be a godmother in the canonical, legal sense, but that she would gladly participate in the ceremony as a "spiritual" godmother. And that is what happened. The baptism took place in Rome, with Bishop Hnilica presiding, and Mother Teresa became a spiritual godmother to little Cristel. During the ceremony the baby girl received the names Cristel, Maria Chiara, and Teresa.

Two years later, in August 1988, some of my friends told me the very moving story of a young wife from an area near Lake

Bracciano (northwest of Rome) who had given birth to quintuplets. As often happens in such cases, the babies were kept in incubators for varying lengths of time. For all practical purposes, they were saved by the very great love of their parents and by the doctors' excellent care.

When they finally left the hospital and were brought home, the issue of baptism was raised. "You need to have a great celebration," said the couple's friends. I thought about Mother Teresa again on this occasion. I was sure that once she heard the story, she would be willing to come. As always, I turned to Bishop Hnilica, who spoke to Mother Teresa, and she agreed to come.

The baptism was held in the ancient church of Santa Maria di Galeria in the suburbs of Rome. Each of the quintuplets had different godparents, as required by the Church, but they also each had Mother Teresa as their "spiritual" godmother. Despite her many commitments, Mother Teresa gave an entire afternoon to the occasion.

Afterward she told me: "I was moved when I heard the story of these babies. They were rescued by their parents' great love and the generous dedication of the doctors who fought long and hard for the lives of these little ones. It was so wonderful, and it touched me. For fifty years I have devoted energy to rescuing sick and abandoned babies. I know how much joy there is when we succeed in seeing them live. For that reason I wanted to participate in the celebration, agreeing to be present at the baptism as a spiritual godmother of these little ones. I have prayed for them and asked Jesus to protect them always."

•

Chapter Ten

GOD IS HERE

Jesus commanded me to dedicate my life to the poor and specifically emphasized that I needed to concern myself with the poorest of the poor—those who have nothing and no one—the rejected, abandoned, and forgotten."

Whenever she spoke of her mission, Mother Teresa always emphasized the "main characteristic" of the task that Jesus had entrusted to her. She reasserted that it was a "command" and not just a piece of good advice, an inspiration, or a suggestion. It was a command that she initially tried to evade, but Jesus was immovable: "This is what you must do."

The Home for the Dying

In obedience to the phrase that Jesus used, "the poorest of the poor," the activities of Mother Teresa and her Missionaries of Charity expanded over time. "The poorest of the poor" are not only those who are completely deprived of means by which to sustain themselves but also those who have extreme poverty in their spiritual lives, especially in our day, and these poor are sometimes the worst off of all.

Mother Teresa took Jesus' command literally, and at the beginning directed her attention to those forms of poverty that are the most obvious for people on the lowest rungs of society. These are the people whom no one thinks about and who are not worth anything because their lives are already over, so to speak, and any help would be useless.

One of the first things she did was to open a home for the dying. It was an extraordinary and brilliant idea that made the essence of the Christian vision of life something tangible and concrete.

Calcutta, where Mother Teresa lived and where she had begun her missionary activity, was the most populated city in India. Once that nation got its independence in 1947, thousands of refugees arrived in Calcutta who were not able to find accommodations and who wandered around the city, especially in the suburbs. They became victims of hunger and disease. Every day dozens of poor people without a roof over their heads fainted from weakness and collapsed to the ground. Many of them never got up again and died in the street.

Hospitals and government agencies tried to help these people, but given the large number of cases—which were, in fact, increasing—they succeeded in doing very little. They tried to assist the people who could be rescued, but they abandoned the elderly, the sickest, and those who would die even if they were brought to the hospital.

These destitute people, then, were left to the mercy of their miserable destinies. When their strength left, they fell to the ground and dragged themselves to the side of the street. Ignored by passersby, they waited to die.

In the Temple of the Goddess Kali

"One time as I was leaving my house," Mother Teresa recounted, "I came upon a man lying on the sidewalk who was dying. I went to the hospital nearby to ask for help, but they refused to take him in as a patient because they said they had no room and the man would die anyway. I was bewildered by their response. For me, that man was a son of God; he could not be abandoned in the middle of the street in his condition. So I went to a pharmacy to get some medicine, but when I returned after a few minutes, he was already dead. He had died breathing in the dust of the street.

"How shameful! I felt partly responsible. I said to myself that I needed to do something. Then I got the idea of opening a house where we could assist these dying people by letting them see a human face, a person near to them who would smile tenderly to let them know that they did not need to be afraid because they were going to their Father's house.

"My idea was fully embraced by the sisters, and it happened that we found a building where we could care for the dying. I went to an administrator in the city and then to the director of health services. 'Give me at least one room,' I requested. Everyone was in favor of my initiative, so different proposals were discussed. Of course, I had neither funds nor ways of resolving the issue by myself. In the end they decided to give me permission—although provisional—to use the hostel for pilgrims that was connected to the temple of the goddess Kali because it had been empty for some time. I called the house 'Nirmal Hriday,' which means 'Pure Heart' and refers to the Immaculate Heart of Mary.

"We started working immediately. However, great difficulties arose. The house was located at the sacred site of the Kali Temple, which enjoys great popularity and is serviced by four hundred priests. Someone told them that the sisters and I had come there to convert them to Christianity. There were debates and pro-tests. Many people aligned themselves against us while others supported our work.

"One political leader publicly promised that he would chase us out, whatever the cost. He came to visit so that he could build his arguments against us. He toured the rows of patients, observing the sisters doing their work. He was shocked when he observed what the sisters were doing because he could see that they were lovingly dedicated to these desperate people. The sisters cleaned the wounds of their worn-out bodies and spoon-fed those who were not able to feed themselves. When he finished his tour, he told the people outside who were waiting for him, 'I promised to chase these sisters out of here, and I will do it, but only when you bring your mothers, your wives, your sisters, and your daughters to do the work that these women are doing. In the temple you have a goddess of stone; here you have living goddesses.'

"Subsequently, a priest of the goddess Kali came down with tuberculosis, a disease that is still very much feared in India. He found acceptance from us, and we cared for him attentively. Every day one of his colleagues would visit him, and they were very impressed by our behavior toward the priest and the other patients. Little by little, all the priests of the goddess Kali became our friends and supporters. The hostility ceased, and we were able to continue our work in peace."

Pope John Paul II's Tears

She told other stories about that house. "The Home for the Dying Destitute is one of the undertakings that is closest to my heart. It has become a sacred place because every day in that house, there is genuine contact between heaven and earth. Many people, in fact, end their human experience there to be united with the Father. In helping these people, we experience the presence of God in a palpable way.

"When they are taken in, dying people are frightened, desolate, and hopeless. But seeing our calm and serene faces bent over them with love and tenderness, they listen to our words of faith and hope, and end their lives with a smile on their lips.

"One day the sisters found a man on the street whose body was covered with sores filled with maggots. He was at the end of his life. I began to wash him and give him medicine. With his eyes half opened, he followed my every movement. Little by little, a great serenity appeared on his face. 'Are you suffering?' I asked. 'Yes, very much,' he answered in a faint voice. He added, 'But I am happy. I have always lived without a home, just like an animal. Surrounded by so much care and love now, I will die like an angel.'

"Another time the sisters brought in a woman who did not even look human any longer and had no vital signs. I washed her and took care of her as I spoke softly to her. Then I had her lie down on a cot. At that point she took my hand and smiled. I had never seen such a beautiful smile. In a whisper she murmured, 'Thank you,' and closed her eyes forever.

"Pope John Paul II, during his trip to India in 1986, came to visit our home for the dying. He stayed for a long time. He wanted to spoon-feed some old people and was present at the death of three people. For the whole time he was there, he did not say one word. He was quite moved, and tears welled up in his eyes."

The Gift of Love

I asked Mother Teresa, "How many people have died in your arms in that home?"

"I do not really know," she answered. "Perhaps thousands. The majority of the dying people we take in off the street to try to save are in desperate straits, and they generally do not recover."

"After seeing so many people draw their last breath, have you become accustomed to death?"

"It is impossible to remain indifferent in the face of death. It is the most important moment in a person's life. Every time someone dies in my arms, it is as if Jesus dies. I help each one with the love I have for God."

This home for the dying has become a sacred place. From the very beginning, Mother Teresa considered it one of her most treasured works. When speaking about that house, she always repeated, "God is here."

The lower-class house of white plaster is always open. It does not even have any doors. Anyone can enter, and often young men and women join the sisters to help the patients to die with smiles on their faces. The dying are brought by ambulances, wagons, and hand-drawn carts. The sisters wash them, medicate them, and watch over them. The cots are arranged in three rows in subdued lighting.

In one corner there is a statue of Our Lady wearing a crown made of several rings of gold. They are nose rings from women who died in this place. Mother Teresa was the one who thought of the idea for the crown and had it made. Placing it on Our Lady's head, she said, "Those who had nothing on earth have given a gold crown to the Mother of God." The statue is draped with a ribbon that has a medal attached to it, the Padma Shri medal, a very prestigious award that the governor of India gave to Mother Teresa in 1962.

One day an English lord visited Nirmal Hriday. When he left, he said, "Now the expensive clothes I am wearing are burning my skin."

In 1973 a chemical engineer from India gave Mother Teresa a large new building that originally had been intended to house the central laboratories of his company. Many people thought she might transfer the dying to this building, but she did not. "I will never abandon the home near the temple of Kali," she said.

She called the new building "Prem Dan," which means "Gift of Love," and she reserved it for those who have the best chance of surviving and recovering. Prem Dan is a type of hospital where needy people sometimes stay for long periods of time. They are discharged only when they are able to walk on their own and can provide sustenance for themselves. ✧

Chapter Eleven

•

HER FAVORITE SONS
AND DAUGHTERS

When she was later traveling around the world, Mother Teresa carried a red cotton bag, a handbag for her small "necessities." Even though that shabby-looking bag seemed to be of no value in the least, she treated it very carefully, as if it were a family memento or a gift from a very dear person. She actually had affection for it. The reason that Mother Teresa guarded that small cotton bag so zealously was that it had been made for her by her favorite children, those with leprosy.

The cloth, in fact, had been woven with great difficulty by the mutilated hands of a person among the numerous leprosy victims that she was helping who had been stricken with that terrible disease. It was then cut and sewn by other hands that were also disfigured by leprosy. Thanks to Mother Teresa, these people had been able to find rewarding work that allowed them a way to earn a living with dignity.

Condemned to a Life of Shame

Leprosy is a horrible disease, and until treatment became more widely available, it was feared as one of the worst diseases that could afflict a person. It does not condemn someone to an early death, as cancer or AIDS can, but without treatment it condemns its victims to a life of shame and branding. Because it is contagious, a person who contracts leprosy and has no access to treatment is immediately separated from society. In ancient times someone with leprosy had to live far from inhabited locations and have a bell tied to his or her ankle. The sound of the bell warned healthy people to get away. Today the bells have been abolished, but in many poverty-stricken countries, those with leprosy continue to be marginalized.

It is estimated that there are four million people with leprosy in the world, and three million of them live in India. In the 1950s in Calcutta, where Mother Teresa chose to begin her mission of love, there were more than half a million people with the disease, which today is called "Hansen's disease."

Without treatment leprosy is progressive, causing permanent damage to the skin, nerves, limbs, and eyes, and often shortening and deforming fingers and toes. Since it is impossible for those with leprosy to find work, they have no means of obtaining the necessities of life to sustain themselves. Chased away from human company and even their own families, people with leprosy have always been part of the great host of "the poorest of the poor." From the very beginning of her missionary work, Mother Teresa began to take care of them and early on showed her partiality for them. One of her favorite sayings was this: "There are no lepers. There is just leprosy, and it can be cured."

When I was in India, I went to visit those with leprosy who gather at the outskirts of the large cities or in country areas that are remote from the urban centers. I always experienced a terrible revulsion. It was disturbing and distressing to see those people— young and old, women and men, babies and adolescents—all disfigured by the disease, often repulsive to look at because leprosy had eaten away their noses and their faces. I had promised the missionaries who accompanied me that I would not display any reaction and that I would conduct myself as though I were among healthy people, but I am not sure that I succeeded. The people smiled at me and were happy to see me. They greeted me and extended their hands to me, which were almost always deformed. I would smile too and clasp their stumps, but I believe that my face was deadly pale. Leprosy leaves a profound impression that arouses an instinctive, deep rejection. Nevertheless, people with leprosy were Mother Teresa's favorite sons and daughters.

Rejected by Their Families

Working with those with leprosy demonstrates a choice based on the highest kind of altruism. Only souls of the most intense spirituality, of visceral ardent love, succeed in living together normally with these afflicted people. It is indeed a heroic choice.

St. Francis of Assisi made his decisive choice for conversion by embracing a man with leprosy. Mahatma Gandhi said that those with leprosy were God's favorites. It was inevitable that after choosing the mission of total love for the poor in India, Mother Teresa would also become involved in the serious problem of leprosy in that nation. That work did not happen immediately, at the beginning of her mission, but only after she had gained an understanding of her new undertaking and solid experience to carry it out.

"In 1957," she told me, "five people with leprosy came and knocked at our door. They belonged to middle-class families. They had held distinguished posts in their careers. However, once their disease was discovered, they were cast out, and no one wanted to see them anymore. They could not even return to their families. In order to survive, they were forced to beg. They asked us for help, so we took them in.

"Fortunately, at that time we had become friends with a doctor, Dr. Sen, who gave us a hand from time to time in helping to care for the poor. His assistance proved very valuable and providential. He instructed me and my sisters in the treatment of leprosy. And so, almost by chance (but nothing is by chance in the Lord's vineyard), we began our work with these people."

By 1957 Mother Teresa already had nine years of experience behind her in her mission. The congregation she had founded had already been recognized by the Church. It had some structure, a Rule, and some houses.

During her nine years of activity up to that point, Mother Teresa had helped the poor in the slums and those who were dying in the streets of Calcutta, but she had also incorporated a way to include those with leprosy, even if it was only now and then. She listened to their stories, knew their situations, and thought about their problems.

She had certainly sensed, at the core of her being, that these sick people would become her favorites. However, being an extremely practical and realistic woman, she was aware that to truly love them and to succeed in giving them genuine help, she needed to be appropriately prepared. From early on she began to prepare consciously for this particular branch of her charitable work.

She investigated how other religious institutions and social agencies dealt with leprosy victims. She wanted to know what they did, how they did it, and what results they got. She reflected on the situation, sought counsel, and then formulated her plans.

"Touching the Body of Christ"

Her basic approach to all her activities was always the same, and it flowed out of her faith convictions. For her, people afflicted by leprosy were children of God just like all other human beings. Jesus died on the cross for them as well. Being marked by such intense suffering and by such a difficult situation in life, they were participating—and more so than many other Christians—in the mystery of the redeeming passion of Jesus that continues through the Mystical Body of Christ.

"I know," she affirmed, "that when I touch a person with leprosy who oozes stench from every part of his or her body, I am touching the body of Christ just as I do when I receive Communion and make contact with the Body of Christ that is really present under the appearance of bread in the Eucharist."

In her spiritual vision of the world, victims of leprosy are very precious people. As children of God and human beings, they have a right to dignity, to respect, to civilized living conditions, and to the possibility of having a job, a family, and social relationships— all the things that society denies them by marginalizing them and restricting them to filthy ghettoes.

There were a variety of leprosy colonies in Calcutta, but they took care of only a very small portion of those afflicted. The majority of those with leprosy remained in their homes, attempting to conceal their disease from everyone. For Mother Teresa, that was the most delicate aspect of the problem. Those people were a dangerous source of contagion, and they were hindering medical oversight of the disease. Mother Teresa decided that she needed to find these "anonymous" victims in hiding and convince them to get medical help.

Mother Teresa began her work using a novel approach. She was acquainted with a Belgian doctor near Madras, Dr. Frans Hemerijckx, who had developed a method of treating leprosy on a large scale. Using mobile leprosy clinics that were appropriately equipped, he brought medicine to the victims in their homes. He succeeded in reaching a rather considerable number of these "secret" leprosy victims this way. It was a practical, effective method, so Mother Teresa decided to adopt it in Calcutta.

She talked about it with some government doctors and convinced them to work with her and her sisters. The mobile leprosy clinics became a specialty of the Missionaries of Charity. The first ones were blessed by Archbishop Perier of Calcutta, whose support attracted interest and attention in the media. Newspaper reports highlighted the novelty and effectiveness of the approach. The work immediately became accepted and very popular. Because of it, the sisters helped tens of thousands of leprosy victims and succeeded in curing many of them.

Constant Battles

Mother Teresa did not overlook other kinds of help for leprosy victims, such as the traditional treatments used in leprosy sanitariums. She availed herself fully of those means, especially for the recovery of those whose disease was the most advanced, so that they could have all the appropriate assistance necessary.

One day Mother Teresa learned that the governing authorities had decided to designate an area on the outskirts of Calcutta as a new residential zone. One of her leprosy houses was in that zone. The authorities ordered her to close her house there and leave the area. No one would ever move there and live next to such a house because the place was considered infected by a disease that everyone greatly feared.

Mother Teresa was indignant. She was concerned about her people and wondered what would become of them. She was aware that any kind of resistance would be futile because when it was a question of economic interest, the government could not be stopped. Defending this house was a battle that was lost at the front end, so she decided to seize the occasion to raise public awareness.

She went to the minister of health, after having, of course, informed the newspapers of her plan, to plead the cause of the victims she was helping. She was already a very popular figure in Calcutta, so the press lined up on her side, extolling her humanitarian activity. Simultaneously, she launched a campaign to collect funds to open a new house for those with leprosy. She called the campaign "Leprosy Collection Day." She sent her sisters and lay friends around the city with containers that had signs saying, "Touch a leper with your compassion."

The response was extraordinary. Money poured in from everywhere. The minister, seeing such interest from the public and the sympathy that Mother Teresa was evoking, was not able to ignore the situation. He officially offered her a large plot of land where she could house the leprosy victims who were being evicted from the residential zone. In the end she obtained better accommodations for her favorite sons and daughters than they had previously.

In 1958 Mother Teresa opened an important center for those with leprosy in Titagarh, an industrial quarter on the outskirts of Calcutta. For a long time, that place had become a refuge for many suffering from the disease. It consisted of a conglomeration of shacks that were in unimaginable states of decay in a marshy area. With leprosy also come trouble and criminal activity. No one, not even the police, would dare to venture into that zone, where violence was the law and atrocious crimes were often committed.

Mother Teresa went to visit that ghetto. She could see the tragic condition of those poor people. The disease was being spread even to newborns. In her usual surprisingly decisive manner, she determined that the area needed to be cleaned up and immediately began taking appropriate action. Given the extreme difficulties due to the physically unhealthy atmosphere and the danger of the gangs entrenched in that area, she assigned the male branch of her congregation that she had recently founded (the Missionaries of Charity Brothers) to do the job.

As always, the beginning was rough. Recalling the great love that Gandhi had for those with leprosy, Mother Teresa wanted the center to be called "Gandhiji Prem Nivas," which means "Gandhi's Gift of Love." The area was disinfected, and new lodgings and streets were built; other new buildings included a rehabilitation center, a hospital, shops, and restaurants.

An Oasis from a Wilderness

Her greatest masterpiece on behalf of victims of the disease, however, was Shanti Nagar, meaning "City of Peace," a self-sufficient village where those with leprosy live as free citizens without the fear of being chased by police or the humiliation of being marginalized.

The village is about two hundred miles from Calcutta, near the border of the state of Bihar in eastern India. The area was at one time an uninhabited wilderness. In 1961 the chief minister of Bengal, Bidhan Chandra Roy, an important Indian politician who was a Communist but also a great admirer of Mother Teresa, wanted to give the diminutive nun and her congregation about thirty-five acres. After ascertaining that the area had plenty of water, Mother Teresa began to cultivate the land and, in a few years, brought forth a little paradise.

She had dreamed of having a small city for her sons and daughters with leprosy in that area, and she succeeded magnificently. Today that wilderness is an oasis of greenery, with tree-lined avenues and flowering gardens. There is also a small lake stocked with fish, and there is also livestock, which provide protein for the inhabitants. Little by little, various buildings went up: a rehabilitation center, a hospital, nursery and elementary schools, and a lot of small brick houses with simple designs that harmonized with the natural surroundings.

The village is under the direction of one of Mother Teresa's sisters. Those with leprosy live in small homes, each of which houses a nuclear family. They work in shops, in the fields, and in raising pigs and chickens. Only the very ill become patients at the hospital. The children benefit from the day-care center and the schools and are under constant medical supervision to detect any possible contamination at the very outset so that it can be dealt with immediately.

The village is practically autonomous. The people grow rice, fruit, and vegetables in the fields for their food. They have also learned to bake bricks for the construction of their homes.

Nothing goes to waste, and everything is recycled. There is even a special piece of equipment to convert chicken excrement to an odorless and colorless gas that is used for cooking. Many healthy people also live in the village—some of whom are volunteers and who by their presence and daily association with the leprosy victims eliminate every kind of marginalization, restoring to them the dignity of human beings who have rights.

One day Mother Teresa, comparing the evils in India to those of rich Western nations, said to me, "Those with leprosy may appear disfigured but, like the poor, they are wonderful people who are capable of great love. Leprosy is without doubt a terrible disease to be burdened with, but it is not as terrible as feeling deprived of love or unwanted or abandoned. The extreme loneliness that I have found among some people in rich nations is worse than leprosy.

"A while ago a very wealthy man came to our house in New York. He said to me, 'Please come visit me. I am half blind, my wife is becoming mentally ill, and our children are traveling around the world and never think about us. My wife and I are dying of loneliness. We want to hear the sound of a human voice around us.' That man was living in a beautiful home and had a lot of money, but he was unhappier than a poor leper in India."

•

Chapter Twelve

THE MIRACULOUS MEDAL

Mother Teresa loved Jesus, but she also loved the mother of Jesus, the Virgin Mary. In his human body, Jesus came to us through Our Lady, the Mother of God. Jesus and his mother are united.

Mother Teresa was a practical, down-to-earth person. She always held to the essential concepts of faith and drew out their practical implications. Her devotion toward and her understanding of Our Lady—the mother of Jesus, the woman who was assumed body and soul into heaven—were proportional to her great faith and love for Jesus.

Prayers and Signs

One day she said to me, "I am always thankful to my earthly mother and to my true mother, Our Lady. When I was a young girl in Albania, I would walk with my mother, who would say to me, 'My little girl, always be guided by Our Lady, who is your true mother. Try to always have her hold your hand the way I am holding your hand now.' From that time on, I understood that my real mother is Our Lady.

"I have not forgotten that truth throughout my life, and I have acted accordingly. I have always been guided by my heavenly mother. Before making any decision, I have always turned to her and she has 'guided' me."

In her spiritual life and her relationship with God, Mother Teresa always aimed at practical results. Her faith was never detached from the realities of life. If she had material needs or problems, she prayed fervently to get specific answers from God. Her approach to the "fatherhood" of God and the "motherhood" of Our Lady was actually quite simple and basic. "God is a father," she would say, "and so he loves me and helps me. Our Lady is a mother, so she understands me and my problems and knows when I need help. I pray to her because I am sure she will help me."

Her prayers were shaped by this practical kind of spirituality in which her certitude of being heard was an indication of her whole-hearted love. Mother Teresa openly and passionately asked for and cherished "physical symbols" that can help keep us in contact with the people we love. She kept the photographs of the children she had rescued who were then adopted. She was attached to "her" rosary—the one she held in her hand every day, many times a day, during her long "conversations" with Our Lady. She liked to visit shrines, and she had a very great devotion for the "miraculous medal," a medal of Our Lady that dates back to 1832.

"Not Happy to Be by Himself"

One night, at the end of a meeting in Rome, I said good-bye because I was returning to Milan the next day. While we were talking, she noticed that I had a gold chain around my neck.

"What is attached to your chain?" she asked.

"Jesus," I answered, taking out the part of the chain that was not visible and showing her a beautiful crucifix. I was sure she would be pleased by that, and, in fact, she gave me a big smile.

But then she said, "Jesus is not happy to be by himself. He likes to be in the company of his mother. When he was crucified, Mary was there at the foot of the cross. They always like to be close to us together." While she was saying this, she took out a small medal of Our Lady from a pocket in her sari. She showed it to me and said, "This is the 'miraculous medal' that St. Catherine Labouré had made after a specific request from Mary." She folded her hands around it, concentrating in prayer. Then she fumbled with her arthritic fingers and succeeded in opening the hoop at the top of the medal and attaching it to my neck chain. "Here," she said, satisfied. "Now the mother and the son are together, and both will protect you."

"Thank you. That is a wonderful gift," I said. I was going to add something else, but she interrupted me and asked, "How many are there in your family?"

"My wife, two children, and my mother-in-law," I replied.

"What are their names?"

I told her their names, and she rummaged around again in the pocket of her sari and took out four medals. She clasped them in her hands, paused to pray, and then gave them to me, pronouncing the name of the person for each medal. I thanked her on behalf of my family members, said good-bye, and took a taxi to the airport.

The Story of St. Catherine Labouré

I was pleased with her gift. I knew that Mother Teresa had a great liking for that medal. It was linked to the story of a humble French nun of the Daughters of Charity who was proclaimed a saint by Pope Pius XII in 1947.

Born in 1806, Catherine Labouré entered the Daughters of Charity, founded by St. Vincent de Paul, when she was twenty-four. While she was a novice in Paris, she had three visions of Our Lady. The first one occurred on the night of July 19, 1830. As she told the story, she was awakened by her guardian angel and told to go to the convent chapel where Our Lady was waiting for her. There she saw a majestic woman seated on a throne near the altar.

The second apparition occurred a few months later on November 27. The Blessed Virgin appeared to Sr. Catherine again in the chapel. This time she was standing, clothed in white silk with a white veil on her head and a mantle of silvery blue. Her feet rested on a globe that was half illuminated, and she was crushing a serpent of a greenish color speckled with yellow. With her arms outstretched, she had rays of light emanating from her hands. Our Lady assigned Catherine the task of having a medal struck with this apparition and of distributing the medal to others.

Catherine confided the two visions to her confessor, who did not believe her. A few weeks later, Our Lady appeared to Catherine for the third time and reproved her for not having the medal struck yet. Catherine talked to her confessor again, and this time he referred the situation to the bishop, and Our Lady's desire was fulfilled.

In 1832 the medal began to be distributed. It was quickly referred to as the "miraculous medal" because through it numerous miraculous signs and healings occurred. Since that time, millions of those medals have been distributed. According to Fr. René Laurentin, a Marian expert and author of a book about Catherine, it has become the most widely distributed medal of all time.

A Bond with Mother Teresa

Mother Teresa was a great supporter of this particular medal. I am not quite sure why. She always carried many of these medals with her and gave them out to everybody. After talking with someone, she often gave them a gift of this medal. She would take a medal, hold it between her hands, pray over it, and then give this small object to the person.

They were wonderful gifts. Whoever knew Mother Teresa knew that they had received something precious, not only because it was a "personalized" medal—Mother Teresa had held it in her hands and prayed for the person who was receiving this gift—but also because this gesture, this partiality, was an act of love on her part and established a kind of emotional bond. Mother Teresa would "bond" herself, so to speak, to the person, considering him or her one of her own, a spiritual son or daughter, one of her co-workers.

Thousands of people from all over the world have received a miraculous medal from her hands. Now that she is dead and lives in heaven, these people know they are protected. She certainly will continue to pray—and with even greater efficacy now.

When I received the medal from Mother Teresa, I considered it a very wonderful gift, precisely because she gave it to me, but nothing more than that. I have always been a bit resistant to devotional excesses and to obsessive attachments to objects, holy pictures, relics, and things of that sort. I have always respected this kind of popular devotion without, however, engaging in it myself. I admire it in humble, simple people because it reveals a pure religious attitude, but I find it annoying in some fanatical people.

I always had great respect for Mother Teresa. I considered her a saint, and every gesture of hers became a point of reflection for me. I asked myself why such an educated woman had such an attachment to a medal, and I thought many times about asking her, but I never did.

I have, however, always worn the medal she gave me. It is made of poor-quality material. I knew that she would never want to distribute a medal made of precious metal, and certainly not of gold. She loved poor things. Considering the medal a precious gift, however, and fearing that it would wear out over time, I had it put into a small oval casing made of gold.

The Attempt on the Pope's Life

In subsequent years I collected reports of significant events connected to this "miraculous medal" and Mother Teresa's devotion to it. I knew that she had hundreds of those medals secretly transported to believers in atheistic Communist countries. They, in turn, secretly distributed them to others.

Bishop Hnilica told me a wonderful story involving the medal. On May 13, 1981, the well-known attack on Pope John Paul II occurred in St. Peter's Square. As he went through the crowd in an open jeep, the pope was struck by a bullet fired by Mehmet Ali Agca. He was taken to the hospital and underwent a five-hour surgery. He was saved by a miracle. That day was the sixty-fourth anniversary of the apparition of Our Lady at Fatima.

During his convalescence, the pope wanted to read the text of the famous "third secret" of Fatima that had not yet been revealed. In that "secret," he recognized himself in the prophecies of the things that were to happen. The doctor who had operated on him explained to him that something quite mysterious had occurred in his wounded abdomen. The bullet had followed a zig-zag path and avoided the vital organs. The pope believed he had been saved through the direct intervention of the Virgin Mary, later affirming many times in public that although one hand fired the gun, another hand guided the bullet.

He began a special mission connected to the message of Fatima. In the 1917 apparition at Fatima, Our Lady had predicted that there would be an atheistic Communist movement and that there would be a second world war. Mary had asked that the pope, in concert with all the bishops in the world, consecrate Russia to her Immaculate Heart to prevent that nation from spreading its errors throughout the world.

For various reasons the consecration requested by Our Lady never took place. The predictions of the Blessed Virgin came to pass almost to the letter: World War II occurred, atheistic Communism in Russia spread to many other nations, and finally, the attempt on the pope's life as described in the third secret took place.

Pope John Paul II, the victim of the attempt, determined to carry out Our Lady's request, and he decided to consecrate Russia on March 25, 1984, the Feast of the Annunciation. To prepare for the event, he sent letters to all the bishops, inviting them to unite themselves with him spiritually on that date.

A Bold Plan

"When Mother Teresa heard about the plan for this event," Bishop Hnilica told me, "she had an inspiration—another one of her astounding ideas. She told me that she needed someone to go to Russia to put a miraculous medal inside the Kremlin. She seemed to want to consecrate the capital of atheism to Our Lady by this gesture, and she asked me if I could help her carry out her project.

"I told her that I was actually the least suitable person to do such a thing, because in Eastern European countries I was considered Communism's number-one enemy, and I had been condemned to death in Czechoslovakia because of my anti-Communist activity there. It was impossible for me to enter the Soviet Union, but I was ready to embark on that adventure if she wanted to help me through prayer.

"Mother Teresa began to arrange the trip. She did everything. She had a good rapport with the Russian consul in Calcutta. I don't know what she told him, but she got me a visa to enter the Soviet Union.

"I arranged to be in Moscow on March 25 of that year during the Feast of the Annunciation when the pope would be consecrating Russia to the Immaculate Heart of Mary. She wanted me to be inside the Kremlin, praying in spiritual union with the pope at the very time that he would be leading the prayer of consecration in Rome, and to deposit one of the famous miraculous medals there.

"I don't know for sure if Mother Teresa shared her plan with Pope John Paul II. There was a trust between them, a kind of harmony of purpose, so I believe she did tell him. In any case, when she gave me the medal to take to the Kremlin, she told me that it had been blessed by the pope.

"In the middle of February, I left Rome for Calcutta and took a trusted colleague with me. Mother Teresa wanted to prepare for the expedition with a lot of prayer. For a month she and I prayed together so that everything would go as we intended. She asked her sisters to pray for an unnamed 'special intention.' Apart from the two of us, no one knew what we were about to do. Mother Teresa had prepared the visas to enter the Soviet Union through the Russian consul and had obtained the plane tickets. My colleague and I were going to pose as two tourists going back to Rome from Calcutta via Moscow, and we would be staying in Moscow for three days to visit the museums there.

"On March 23 Mother Teresa accompanied us to the Calcutta airport. When I said good-bye, she was moved. She clasped my hands affectionately and wanted to give me her rosary.

"The trip was peaceful. We arrived in Moscow at 4:00 a.m. on March 24. The customs official had doubts about my true identity. When I gave him my passport, he started asking a whole series of questions. I pretended not to understand. My passport, of course, was Italian, and I did not want him to know that I could speak Russian. The soldier continued asking questions in Russian, and I continued to say in Italian that I did not understand. Clearly, he had his suspicions. Then he started making a series of phone calls, but it was 5:00 a.m. and no one was answering.

"I was waiting outside his office; it was fifteen degrees below zero. I started to become concerned, so I took Mother Teresa's rosary out of my pocket and began to pray. I could already see myself in Siberia, but I had a lot of faith in Mother Teresa's prayers. I was also repeating, 'Lord, your will be done.' When the soldier came back, he tried to ask me with gestures if the passport was mine. I nodded my head yes. In the end, he stamped my passport and sent me away.

"My colleague and I went to the hotel and started visiting the city unobtrusively, each of us on our own. We asked how we could get into the Kremlin. Through an odd set of circumstances, the Kremlin was open to tourists precisely during those days."

The Kremlin is a citadel inside Moscow that is surrounded by walls. It is a kind of fortress that covers sixty-eight acres. In the past it was the secular and religious center of the city. In fact, the imperial palaces are there as well as some of the most important churches in Moscow, like the Cathedral of the Assumption. After the Bolshevik Revolution in 1917, these churches were closed and made into museums.

"The plan that I had agreed to with Mother Teresa was that on the morning of March 25, when the pope began the ceremony for the consecration of Russia, I would visit the Kremlin as a tourist and stop in the cathedral. Pretending to be interested in the precious art treasures there, I would linger in prayer and try to place the miraculous medal Mother Teresa had given me in an inconspicuous location."

In the Heart of the Kremlin

"I was quite afraid that morning," he continued. "Fortunately, other tourists were visiting the Kremlin, so being in the middle of a large crowd, I felt somewhat protected. I visited some palaces, stopped in at the Cathedral of the Archangel, and then I entered the Cathedral of the Assumption. I looked around closely to see where I could put the medal.

"Even though it had become a museum, the church had been preserved and kept up very well. According to the description of one of the guides, the thrones there were the original thrones on which the czar, the czarina, and the patriarch used to sit during religious ceremonies. The patriarch's throne was in the middle. I decided to put the medal under that throne, praying that the patriarch of Moscow could soon return to perform religious services in that place.

"Taking advantage of a moment when I was alone in that museum-church, I focused on celebrating Mass in secret. I did the consecration with a bread crumb and a drop of wine that I had brought with me. It was an intensely emotional and religious moment for me. It had been seventy-six years since the Eucharist had been celebrated in that place. Then, very slowly, I approached the throne of the patriarchs. I noticed a small crack in the wooden floor, so I placed the miraculous medal there. I stayed a bit longer, praying, and then I went back to the hotel where my colleague was waiting for me. We left for Italy that afternoon."

It was an extraordinary adventure, worthy of such amazing people as Mother Teresa and Bishop Hnilica. Today in Russia, religion is not forbidden. If anyone goes to check that throne, one might still find the medal that certainly protected the cathedral and guided events until the fall of the great atheistic Communist empire.

Remo Gessi's Adventure

A few months after Mother Teresa's death, I met a fellow journalist in Trieste, Remo Gessi, who told me an extraordinary story about a miraculous medal that he had received from Mother Teresa.

An athletic, cultured, and educated man who was an expert in economics, Remo belonged to an illustrious family. His great-grandfather, Romolo Gessi, was the famous nineteenth-century explorer who was a friend and colleague of the legendary Gordon Pascià. His grandfather, Felice, was also an explorer. He has a son named Romolo who, like his great-grandfather, is an orchestra director, while his daughters, Paola and Federica, now graduated and married, are well-known television personalities in Italy.

"I met Mother Teresa in 1988," he told me. "It was a very difficult time for me. I was in a tough situation. The doctors had given me only a few months to live. I had been sick for about five years. It had all started in the summer of 1983, when I became aware of a mole on my right arm five centimeters away from my underarm. I was not happy about it, so I went to my doctor in Trieste. 'It's probably nothing,' he said. However, he was wise to do further tests to make sure it wasn't malignant melanoma.

"I went through clinical tests in Trieste, but the results were not clear. They told me there was a 50 percent chance that it was malignant. I went to the top Italian doctor in the area, Dr. Natale Cascinelli, at the Center for Tumors in Milan. She confirmed it was malignant and operated on me on December 3.

"The outcome was excellent, especially since Dr. Cascinelli did not prescribe any follow-up treatments. She said it was a first-stage cancer, so the timeliness of the intervention had warded off any complications.

"However, four years later the tumor came back. In the meantime I had taken no precautions. I had continued boating, swimming, and being in the sun as I had always done. In 1987 I began to notice itchy spots on my arm as well as swelling. I immediately went to Milan, and Dr. Cascinelli performed another surgery. She said it was a relapse and that the cancer had metasta-sized. I was shocked. The doctor was quite worried about it too. In fact, I was in trouble after three months. Other tumors formed, and I was operated on again, but it was of no use. The metastasis led to tumors on my neck, my back, my chest, and my abdomen. I underwent another surgery that did not help.

"Now all hope was gone. Cascinelli recommended that I go to America to see a leading expert in that field, Dr. Charles M. Balch. "Even though I was very sick, I continued working. I was traveling a lot. One day, on a plane from Trieste to Rome, I met Mother Teresa. She had been in Udine for a conference, and on her return trip, it so happened that I was seated next to her."

Hope for a Miracle

Continuing his story, he said, "Before takeoff there was a con-stant stream of people who wanted to meet her, shake her hand, and entrust this or that sick person to her. I could not help over-hearing, but I did not for one minute think of telling her about my illness.

"When the plane took off, I was alone next to her, and we began to speak in English. We talked about the conference in Udine. She could somehow see into my soul, however, and noticed that I was quite worried.

"Looking into my eyes, she asked, 'What is going on?' Then I told her about my problem. She wanted me to tell her the whole story. I told her about the tumors, about the unexpected surger-ies, and about the trip I was going to take to Houston, Texas. She listened very attentively. At the end she told me that I should have faith and said the ordinary things that people say in similar circumstances. Then, as if moved by a sudden inspiration, she turned to the sister sitting on the other side of her and asked her something. The nun gave her a small medal. Mother Teresa took it in her hands, closed her eyes, and prayed for about a minute. Then she gave me the small medal, saying, 'Wear it around your neck, and do not ever take it off. Let's hope Our Lady will do a miracle for you.'

"She used the very word 'miracle.' As I reflected about it later, it occurred to me that she had perfectly understood the gravity of my situation. The doctors, after three surgeries, could no longer do anything for me, but my body was full of tumors. They would cut away in one area, and the cancer would return in another. It is strange that she said, 'Let's hope Our Lady will do a miracle for you' because it was clear that only a miracle could save me.

"When we landed in Rome, I said good-bye to her, but I realized that this contact had unexpectedly changed my life. When I got home, I put the medal she gave me around my neck, and I put it on with a lot of faith, a faith that had been 'transfused' into me from her. I was not the same person I was before. My wife, Nadilla, noticed it immediately. I was no longer hopeless. I had found the strength to fight back. There was also a strange peace. I no longer thought of dying but had instead a great desire to live peacefully and well, no matter for how long."

Still Healthy and Happy

Then Gessi told me the rest of his story. "I decided to do everything the doctors had recommended, but I did it with absolute detachment, as if I were already healthy. I went to Houston and met with Dr. Balch, who ordered treatments. I toured the United States with my wife for a month because I wanted a vacation with her. When I got back to Italy, I did the prescribed treatment, continuing to live as though healthy, without the least bit of worry. Then an amazing thing happened. The cancer stopped; the metastasis disappeared. Little by little, the swollen lymph glands all over my body began to shrink and then became invisible. No new tumors appeared, so I did not need any surgeries. Every six months I go to the doctors for a checkup, and they are always astounded. Everything vanished; the illness went into remission, and there is no longer any cancer.

"Was it Mother Teresa? Was it Dr. Balch's treatments? It's hard to say. I only know that other people who had the same condition who were with me in Houston were not helped by the treatment, and unfortunately, after a short time, they died. I continue to be alive twenty-three years later, and I am as healthy as if I had never had cancer.

"In 2010, on the hundred-year anniversary of Mother Teresa's birth, my wife and I celebrated my eightieth birthday and our fiftieth wedding anniversary."

•

Chapter Thirteen

FAMILY TRAGEDIES

Mother Teresa never spoke about her family. When people asked her specific questions about her childhood or early youth, they received brief, generic, almost evasive answers. Often she did not respond at all, for whatever unknown reason, and gave the impression that she did not want to discuss the topic.

Her silence and restraint, however, were actually concealing a drama. During our meetings I also tried to ask about her family, but I became aware that the questions caused her pain, so I dropped the issue.

I already knew about her story. I had learned it in 1979 from Lazar, Mother Teresa's brother, after she was awarded the Nobel Peace Prize. She was the subject of discussion in the press after the award, so when Italian journalists discovered that she had a brother in Sicily, we rushed there to interview him. It was there that I learned the sorrowful events of Mother Teresa's family and the reasons for her silence.

Fortunate Children

Mother Teresa was born on August 26, 1910, in Skopje. For many years nearly all journalists reported that she was Slavic, but she was actually Albanian.

Skopje, the capital of Macedonia and an important center today, was under the rule of various countries during its history. It was annexed to Turkey and to Serbia, but it originally was an Albanian city. Most of the inhabitants of Skopje speak Albanian, and Mother Teresa's parents, who considered themselves Albanian, also spoke Albanian.

Her father, Nikola Bojaxhiu, was a capable businessman with a pharmacy degree. He also headed a construction company and had built the first important theater in Skopje. Her mother, Drana (the name of a flower in Albania), came from a well-to-do family. She married young, at the age of fifteen, and was eighteen years younger than her husband. At the age of sixteen, she gave birth to her first daughter, Aga; at eighteen, to Lazar; and at twenty, to Agnes, the future Mother Teresa. The name "Agnes" was quickly replaced at home by the nickname "Gonxha," which means "flower bud." The family lived in a beautiful home with a large flowering garden. There was another house on the garden grounds reserved for visiting guests and relatives.

Skopje's population at that time was primarily Muslim. There was also a large group of Greek Orthodox, but Roman Catholics were few in number. The Bojaxhiu family was part of that small minority. As so often happens with people in the minority, the Bojaxhiu family was proud of their faith and practiced it with enthusiasm, consistency, and zeal. That was especially true of Drana, who had responsibility for the children's education. She was very religious and quite diligent about passing on the faith that she had received from her parents to her children.

The Church Near Home

There was a small church close to the family's home. Every morning, after Nikola left for work, Drana would bring her three children to the church to attend Mass and pray. In the evening when it was getting dark, Drana would gather the family into the living room to say the rosary. This was a very important part of the day, and relatives or guests staying at the guesthouse were also invited to participate.

Drana lived her faith in simple and concrete ways. Obedient to the teaching of the gospel, she was committed to loving her neighbors by doing good deeds. Remembering Jesus' words "As you did it to one of the least of these my brethren, you did it to me" (Matthew 25:40), she made it a habit of going once a week to visit the city's sick and to bring food, provisions, and clothes to the poor. She wanted her children, even when they were young, to accompany her. "You are fortunate children," she would tell them. "You have a beautiful home, food, and clothes. You lack nothing. You should never forget that so many people here are suffering. There are children who have no clothes, and when they get sick, they do not have any medicine to help them get well."

Agnes' Little Friends

Lazar, Mother Teresa's brother, said that the one in the family who followed the advice of their mother the most enthusiastically was the youngest child, Agnes.

"There was a poor widow who had seven children, almost all very young, who lived in a dark, filthy room," he told me.

"Our hearts would break when we went to visit her with our mother. We would see those poor creatures with no real kitchen to speak of and without a bathroom, while each of us had a very nice room and even a bathtub with hot water, which was a rarity in Skopje.

"My sister Aga and I never went willingly to that house, but Agnes was almost always there with those filthy and malnourished children. Before returning home after school, she always went to see her little friends. Then she would return in the late afternoon to eat a snack with them. Of course, she brought all the food herself. When the poor woman died, her seven children practically lived at our house for a while."

Her mother's example must have left a profound impression on little Agnes' heart. Speaking of her own religious vocation, Mother Teresa told me, "I do not know what had the most influence in the unfolding of my vocation: my mother's example of love for the poor or my regular attendance at church."

Political Assassination

The tranquility and serenity of the Bojaxhiu family did not last long. Nikola, the head of the family, was involved in politics. He fought for the rights of the citizens of Kosovo, whose Albanian citizens wanted to remain with Albania.

When Albania gained its independence in 1913, the Bojaxhiu family celebrated. Soon after, however, the country was split apart, and the region of Kosovo was relegated to Yugoslavia. Kosovo wanted to return to Albanian rule, so there were continual pockets of resistance and tension that the troops from Belgrade would squelch with violence. The Slavic troops took aim especially at the most influential people who held sway over the population. Agnes' father, who was esteemed and respected throughout the city, was among that group.

The Slavic authorities began to pursue Nikola Bojaxhiu. They threatened him with retaliation and revenge. They began to sabotage his work through any means possible. His business was subjected to major harassment that brought it to the point of collapse. Nikola Bojaxhiu, however, would not stop his activities. The Slavic authorities, therefore, used extreme measures to eliminate this man, who was nothing but a rebel in their eyes.

"One day," Lazar said, "my father, who was a city councilman, went to Belgrade for a meeting. When he was transported back home in a carriage, he was doubled over with shooting pains. They took him to the hospital, but there was nothing to be done. He died a few hours later of poisoning. He was forty-six years old. No medical document indicated that he had been poisoned, but we knew only too well that he had been eliminated in that manner by the Slavic police for political motives."

The Bojaxhiu family suddenly found itself in very serious financial difficulty. The family business had closed, so the family was in desperate straits. Drana Bojaxhiu, however, did not lose heart. She had three children to raise, ranging in age from nine to thirteen. To feed her children, she courageously began a new commercial enterprise. She sold cloth, carpets, embroidered goods, and other local handicraft items. It was a business that no one thought would succeed, but it yielded enough profit to allow the family to survive with dignity.

Anxious Years

Meanwhile, Agnes was growing. Following her mother's example, she dedicated her spare time to serving the poor. When she was eighteen, her vocation became clear, and Agnes left her family to enter the convent. She became a sister of the Order of Our Lady of Loreto. She went to Ireland first and then to India. After she left her family, she never saw her mother or her sister, Aga, again.

Mother Teresa's family continued living in Skopje until 1934, when they moved to Tirana in Albania. In 1939 Mussolini wanted to use Albania as the launching point for an invasion of the Balkans. When he ordered the invasion, Lazar Bojaxhiu, at age thirty-one, was an army officer and, like many other soldiers, was incorporated into the Italian troops and sent to fulfill his military service in Turin. When the war was over, he decided to stay in Italy.

Meanwhile, resistance forces in Albania were organized into the liberation army under Enver Hoxha. When Tirana was liberated on January 11, 1946, Albania was declared a People's Republic and became part of the Communist block. A new and terrible crucifixion for that country began.

For more than forty years, Mother Teresa's homeland remained under the dictatorship of Enver Hoxha, one of the most ruthless dictators of the twentieth century. In the beginning, to reinforce his own political position with regard to neighboring countries, Hoxha relied on Stalin. When Stalin died and Nikita Khrushchev proposed new directions for the Soviet Union, he broke with the Kremlin and became a friend of Mao Zedong.

Inside his country he had established a reign of terror enforced by a very efficient and cruel secret police. Whoever was suspected of not being loyal to the dictator was eliminated. Toward the end of the 1960s, after he had embraced the methods of the Chinese Cultural Revolution, he killed four hundred party leaders in a matter of a few days and had thirty generals killed in one day. Mother Teresa's own brother, Lazar Bojaxhiu, was an indirect victim of this bloody dictator: Judged as guilty of having served in the Italian army and of betraying Albania, he was condemned to death in absentia.

Mother Teresa was aware of this situation and feared for the safety of her mother and sister in Tirana. They were closely monitored by the secret police because they were related to a traitor condemned to death and to a religious sister. For more than ten years, she had no news about her mother and sister. Finally, a letter arrived—the two women were still alive.

Failed Attempts

The regime, however, was oppressing them. They had permission to write to relatives on the outside only once a month, but every letter had to go through censorship by the state, and every word was monitored. Because of that, Mother Teresa could never be sure what the real situation was for her mother and sister in terms of their daily lives and health. She could surmise from their letters only that they were suffering. Her mother wrote, "I want to see you before I die. That is the only grace I am praying for to the good Lord."

Taking advantage of the important political people she knew throughout the world, Mother Teresa tried in every way she could to get her mother and sister out of Albania. Toward the end of the 1960s, it seemed that her efforts were finally getting positive results.

Albania was allied with China at that time but was tentatively trying to be open to the West. The French government seemed disposed to open up dialogue. The French minister of foreign affairs, Maurice Couve de Murville, who knew Mother Teresa, presented a request to his counterpart in Tirana personally. After some time, the minister of foreign affairs in Albania responded: "Drana and Aga Bojaxhiu do not have the physical health necessary for a trip out of the country." The request had been refused.

Mother Teresa's dream of seeing her mother and sister again had vanished. She suffered very deeply over it; perhaps she wept, but she never talked about it. She offered her suffering to the Lord, as she had always done. Her mother died in 1974, and her sister died two years later.

After their deaths Mother Teresa continued to remain silent about the fate of her family members. She was waiting for the time when she might be useful to her country of origin. In fact, once Hoxha's regime fell, Mother Teresa and her sisters were invited to work among the poor of that nation. They went immediately and enthusiastically. Perhaps she thought specifically of her mother and sister who, through their suffering, had undoubtedly contributed to the liberation of that country.

Mother Teresa was very attached to her parents, who had given her an excellent education. She suffered—first, at the death of her father, and then, because of her mother's situation. She succeeded, however, in finding the strength to forgive, and for that reason, she preferred not to recall her past, much less express her views on what had happened. ❧

•

Chapter Fourteen

THE MYSTERY OF A VOCATION

When did you realize you had a vocation to be a religious sister?" I asked Mother Teresa.

"The calling of the Lord is a mystery," she replied. "Perhaps only when we are in heaven will we be able to know the most profound 'whys' of our lives.

"I believe I perceived an initial call from the Lord about my future state of life when I was around twelve years old. I was living with my family in Skopje. My mother was a very committed Christian, and perhaps her example, her love for the poor, had a decisive influence on me. But being a sister did not appeal to me then, so it was only much later that I responded to the Lord's call. I was eighteen years old when I decided to consecrate myself to him."

A Complex Path

When the media became interested in Mother Teresa, she was already an adult who had founded a religious community, so their attention was focused on her extraordinary works on behalf of the poor. No one took the time to consider her vocation or the spiritual path that she had followed. It seemed that she had always been "Mother Teresa" rather than a woman who had grown into her spiritual identity little by little.

Her vocation had actually been revealed slowly and through a rather complex path. She told me one day: "A vocation arises out of an intimate dialogue between God and a human being that unfolds in the depth of a person's spirit, and it begins at the very first instant of life. God speaks to unborn babies in the womb, and they understand him well." These wonderful statements are very significant because they guided the future Mother Teresa and the many battles she would have to engage in for her vocation.

There was an "initial call," as she phrased it, when she was about twelve that had roots in the example she received from her family, especially her mother. But it was not yet a call to consecrated life. Agnes was a brilliant student at that time, who enjoyed music, dance, and writing poetry. She looked at life with the enthusiasm of a normal young girl who is full of dreams and grand ideals.

Ever since childhood, she had the habit of living in absolute transparency to herself and to the world. She had confidence in God, talked to him, and listened to him. Her statement that "God speaks to unborn babies in the womb, and they understand him well" was typical for her, as was her idea that a vocation "begins at the very first instant of life." Although it "begins" then, it unfolds little by little, and becomes confirmed and clarified through the dialogue between God and the individual.

A Courageous Choice

Agnes' response to that initial call was immediate—the responses of young people are always generous. But things unfolded, as we shall see, in ways that did not seem to be in perfect concordance with the calling. Great difficulties arose concerning Agnes' vocation that she nevertheless was able to resolve with the wisdom of an inspired soul but also with the courage of a lioness.

She was never constrained by fashion, customs, people pleasing, or people's opinions, and she never yielded to compromises. When she realized that obstacles were holding her back from the fundamental goal of her life, she had the strength to change her plans, to make drastic choices, to risk everything to be faithful to that inner conviction that was so clear—her vocation. That is the path by which she became "Mother Teresa."

She never spoke about the travail that lasted many years, but her travail was the fruit of that "intimate dialogue between God and a human being that unfolds in the depth of a person's spirit and begins at the very first instant of life."

At the age of twelve, she was given an orientation through her "dialogue with God." This was even more the case at age eighteen, when she decided to become a sister. Her life in India, however, unfolded in a way that did not harmonize with her initial ideal. Every day that discrepancy became stronger and more jarring, until Sr. Teresa decided to leave her community at the age of thirty-eight—to lay aside her sister's habit and return to the world to start over from the beginning.

Her choice was ill-advised and absurd, according to the thinking of that time. However, she made the choice anyway. If she had not had the courage to do so, perhaps she would have become just a sister who was diligent but unhappy and frustrated—or perhaps something worse.

The Mission of Her Heart

"When I was twelve, I was attending a school that was not Catholic," Mother Teresa told me. "However, in our parish there were very good priests who watched over our souls zealously and diligently. I was a regular attendee of the religious programs in the parish.

"One day a Jesuit missionary in India came to our church to speak about his work in that country. What he said affected me profoundly. My heart was pierced with a great desire to do mission work to collaborate in spreading the kingdom of God. I talked to the Jesuit about it. He advised me, 'Pray to know God's will.'

"The thought of doing missionary work continued to haunt me for a long time. I knew, though, that to fulfill that desire, I would need to become a sister because only sisters could do missionary work. I did not want to take vows at that time, so I gave up on the idea of India."

Young Agnes Bojaxhiu responded negatively to that first gentle call. However, her response was not a complete refusal. Agnes was not afraid of the difficulties and sacrifices that this calling would entail. She was not closing in upon herself for selfish reasons. She was hesitant merely because her desire to go into the mission field seemed closely tied to having to become a sister, and she did not want to shut herself up in a convent.

Mother Teresa had always been a courageous woman, even since childhood. By the age of twelve, she had gone through a terrible period of her life. Her father had been dead for three years, and her mother had been forced to work hard to maintain the family. Even though she was so young, Agnes helped her mother to provide for many daily necessities. She had learned to be energetic and independent.

Her desire to go to India fit together exactly with her energy and her will to do it. She wanted to collaborate actively with other missionaries to spread the kingdom of God. She thought it would be a very active life full of projects, adventures, dangers, and journeys. She did not see how all of that could happen if she chose convent life.

She probably did not really understand religious life. She was attending a school that was not Catholic. The good priests at church were the ones taking care of her spiritual life, and she and her mother would visit the poor and the sick. However, in telling the story of her childhood, Mother Teresa never spoke about sisters. Perhaps in the primarily Muslim city of Skopje, sisters were rare. This could be the reason that young Agnes firmly decided at that time not to enter the convent.

Letters from Fr. Anthony

Agnes continued living a normal life. The inner calling, though, that impelled her to want to collaborate in spreading the kingdom of God in mission countries did not abate.

A few years passed. Agnes grew. "She was a pretty girl," her brother, Lazar, commented. "She was a sensitive girl who loved music and played the mandolin and the piano."

Young girls in her parish took part in the Sodality of Mary that was led by Jesuits. Agnes came to know some of these men who went to India for missionary work and were carrying out their work in Bengal. They did not forget their friends in Skopje and stayed in contact through letters. One in particular, Fr. Anthony, would send one or two letters a week summarizing the work he and his colleagues were doing.

These missionaries were working in the district of Noakhali, one of the most inaccessible regions of India. It is a marsh area of small islands scattered in the Ganges River delta, where at the time, 2.5 million people lived in an area of 37 square miles. These poverty-stricken people lived in filthy huts reachable only by boat or buffalo-drawn barges.

Fr. Anthony's letters were written with passion and communicated the joy and pride of being a missionary of Christ. When his letters arrived, they were immediately shared among the Catholic youth in Skopje, who read them avidly. Some of them were even published in the newsletter of the Sodality of Mary.

Agnes read these letters too and was enthusiastic about them. The messages from Fr. Anthony kept the desire of doing mission work alive in her heart.

Bengal: Her Goal

The idea became more powerful in Agnes' heart when she was about eighteen years old. She was no longer a child but a woman able to look into her heart with resolution. She realized that the time had come to think concretely about the future and to decide what she wanted to do with her life. She had to choose the right path for herself, and she realized that the only goal she aspired to with her whole heart was to become a missionary. She reflected for a long time. She prayed. When she was sure that she wanted to choose this path, she talked with her mother and her parish priest about it.

Her goal was to go to Bengal. She wanted to work with the Jesuits she knew there—to participate in the life that Fr. Anthony had described so well in his letters and to spread the kingdom of God to the poverty-stricken people living in those marshlands.

The fact remained, however, that a woman who wanted to do missionary work needed to become a sister. Today there are lay missionaries as well, but in the 1920s, only sisters could be missionaries. This time Agnes was quite resolute that since she could not go as a layperson, she would become a sister.

When she asked for information, she was told that the only missionary sisters in Bengal belonged to the religious congregation of Our Lady of Loreto, whose motherhouse is in Dublin, Ireland. If Agnes wanted to be a missionary to Bengal, she needed to go to the motherhouse in Ireland, ask to be accepted into the community, and then request to be sent to India.

She did not want to lose any time. She wrote to Ireland and some time later received an affirmative answer. In the summer of 1928, she left her family and went to Dublin. She joined the community of Our Lady of Loreto and stayed in Ireland less than a year, the time that was required for the sisters in charge of new vocations to evaluate if this young Albanian woman had the qualities to be a good sister. Finally, in February 1929 she was sent to Darjeeling, India, in the Himalayan region, where she would do her novitiate.

Darjeeling is a spectacular area with about a mile and a half of seacoast and a tourist spot where the richest families in India vacation. The community of Our Lady of Loreto has a beautiful house for novices there. The young women aspiring to religious life were required to stay for two years to reflect, meditate, and train for their future convent life. Agnes dedicated herself to studying their Rule and living the spiritual life. These were two very wonderful years for her. She had serenity and peace inside the convent as well as the fantastic natural beauty all around her.

Sister Teresa

At the end of her novitiate, she made her religious vows and said a definitive farewell to the world to become a bride of Christ.

As part of distancing themselves from their past lives, their Rule—according to an ancient custom shared by almost all religious congregations and communities—required that the sisters renounce their birth names and receive new ones. Agnes Bojaxhiu chose the name of a French saint, Thérèse of Lisieux, also known as Thérèse of the Child Jesus. Agnes had been fascinated by this saint, who died at the age of twenty-four. She had read her biography and was struck by the fact that, despite remaining shut up in a cloistered convent, Thérèse was proclaimed "Patron of Missions" by the Church.

That day, after making their vows, the new sisters received their assignments from the superiors. Sr. Teresa was sent to their large high school in Entally (in the central part of Calcutta), with the task of studying for a diploma in education. Her superiors wanted her to become a teacher.

It was an unexpected decision on the part of her superiors that clashed with her desire to do mission work. Sr. Teresa was surprised and perplexed. Reflecting on her recently taken vows, among which was a vow of obedience, she bowed her head, submitted, and prepared to leave.

Her assignment was to teach, but especially to dedicate herself to the spiritual formation of her young female students who were the future women of India—mothers, teachers, managers, directors—women who would affect the quality of progress in India.

The sisters of Our Lady of Loreto had various buildings in Entally, including an English high school and a Bengali high school. Sr. Teresa was sent to the Bengali high school, St. Mary's. Her task was important and very significant. For this reason she threw herself headlong into her new work with all her strength. She was soon doing an excellent job. Her superiors were so pleased with her that after some time, they appointed her as the principal of the school. They also entrusted to her the leadership of the Daughters of St. Anne, a diocesan community of Indian sisters who dressed in blue saris and taught in secondary schools in Bengal.

Teaching in a Wonderful School

The school where young Sr. Teresa taught was in the most beautiful area of Calcutta. It was a westernized area with very beautiful palaces, among which was that of the British governor.

Life at the school was peaceful and pleasant. Sr. Teresa wrote in a letter during this period: "My new life is as a teacher. Our school is wonderful, and I enjoy teaching. I am responsible for an entire school, and I am well liked by many young girls here."

Living within the confines of the school, however, Sr. Teresa never encountered the poor, the "untouchables" of Calcutta, the people dying of hunger and misery in the streets of the city—the ones for whom she had become a religious. She was teaching in large well-lit rooms, praying in a lovely chapel, taking walks around a very beautiful garden, and sleeping in a clean bedroom on a comfortable bed protected from mosquitoes. She wore a lightweight habit and very soft white shoes that allowed her to walk hurriedly through the corridors without making the least noise. However, none of these comforts had touched her spirit in the least. They never led her to forget the missionary ideals that had stirred her heart in Skopje.

At the school in Entally, a group of young women belonged to the Sodality of Mary, which was similar to the group that Sr. Teresa had belonged to in Skopje. These young women pursued various charitable and social activities outside the school. They would, by turns, visit the nearby hospital, Nilratan Sarkar, to comfort the sick, cheer them up, write letters for them, or do small services and errands.

There was also a group of young women who visited the slums every week, the most poverty-stricken areas in the city. These were real ghettos lacking hygienic infrastructures where, together with poverty and moral degradation, the most terrible diseases were spread, including leprosy. People lived in shacks crowded together like sardines—thousand and thousands of dispossessed, so forgotten by everyone that they did not even have registered certificates for birth, marriage, or death.

One of these slums was on the other side of the school walls. It was called "Moti Jhil" ("Pearl Lake"), and Sr. Teresa would have been able to see the wretched hovels if she had looked out the window. This was the place that her students would go to offer their help. When they returned, they would report what they had seen. Their stories were heartbreaking. Sr. Teresa would listen to them in silence without commenting, so no one knows what feelings the students' descriptions enkindled in her heart.

No Visits to the Slums

One fact is certain: While she was teaching, Sr. Teresa never went to visit the poor who were living in the slums. She would have been able to and could have even accompanied the group of her students. Instead, she never went. That fact has been confirmed in a definitive way by Fr. Julien Henry, who was the spiritual director of the school at Entally. Sr. Teresa, who subsequently dedicated all her energy to these poor, never visited them when she was at the school, although a ghetto of misery bordered the building in which she lived.

Why?

It is difficult to discover the answer. It is certain, however, that it was not out of indifference. Perhaps she did not go among the poor because she sensed that it was not quite the right time. Perhaps her very sensitive heart prevented her from facing so much suffering. Or knowing herself so well, she may have been aware that if she went to visit those people even just once, she would not have been able to leave them and would not have returned to fulfill her duty at school. She could not let that happen. She had made a vow of obedience, and her superiors had assigned her to teach.

Who knows how many times she may have thought about those poor people in the secret recesses of her heart, remembering the heartbreaking stories from the girls about the unspeakable suffering in those miserable ghettos? How many times would she have prayed for them, wept, and asked God to give her the opportunity to do something to alleviate their suffering? ∽

Chapter Fifteen

THE NIGHT OF THE "COMMAND"

S r. Teresa was going to turn thirty-six on August 26, 1946. St. Mary's High School, where she was teaching, planned a party for the occasion. Her students loved her, and her birthday was an opportunity to demonstrate their affection and gratitude. It had become the custom that the students returned to school from vacation exactly in time to celebrate her birthday.

Bloody Days

That year, however, the party was not as peaceful and joyful as it had been in the past. India was going through a dramatic time politically. In 1946 that great subcontinent with its more than four hundred million (mostly poor) inhabitants was weary of the British colonial rule that had lasted for more than two centuries. The people wanted their freedom, and they were trying to obtain it, even through bloody revolts.

In the most recent period, the situation had become precarious. Alongside the pacifist movement led by Mohandas Karamchand Gandhi—the charismatic "Mahatma" who was having success at energizing the crowds with his doctrine of nonviolence—many small groups of fanatics, particularly Muslims, took advantage of the political instability to cause uprisings that ended in massacres, looting, fires, and destruction.

The riots were frequent, especially in Calcutta, the most populated city in India, where the poorest Hindus and Muslims in the world were haphazardly crammed in together. The last of the revolts—the bloodiest and most horrifying of the period—occurred on August 16, 1946, and brought terror and death to the impoverished quarters of the city. The Muslim League had declared that day to be "Direct Action Day," inviting all its followers to a demonstration of force against the English and the Hindus. The result was horrific.

That very morning, hundreds of fanatic Muslims came out of their homes armed with clubs, iron bars, and shovels. Rushing wildly through the streets, they mercilessly massacred all the Hindus they encountered, throwing their bodies into canal drains. Shops and homes were set on fire, and in a few hours, the city was enveloped in thick black clouds of smoke.

The police, terrified by such furor, hid themselves and would not respond. Caught unawares, the Hindus suffered greatly at the hands of the Muslims. However, once the initial moment of confusion was over, they organized a counterattack and massacred Muslims.

For twenty-four hours Calcutta was a battleground. According to some reports, that tumultuous day alone saw six thousand people killed. The Hooghly River that runs through the city was full of bloated bodies floating on the water. The guerrilla warfare soon spread to bordering districts in Noakhali and the province of Bihar.

The Moment of Crisis

The echo of the conflict reached the threshold of the peaceful St. Mary's High School. Sr. Teresa had followed the news with anxiety, listening to the reports of the staff at the school. It was appalling. She was horrified to learn of the torture and barbarity that victimized especially the poor and the most defenseless: women, elderly people, and babies. The pain she carried in her heart prevented her that August from enjoying the party for her birthday with her students as she had in previous years. The party took place anyway. Sr. Teresa tried to smile at the gifts her students had given her, but a storm was brewing in her heart. The terrible facts reported about that day led her to reflect not only on the dramatic events happening in India but also on her life.

For some time Sr. Teresa had not felt comfortable with the peaceful life she was living at school. It seemed that something was jammed in the gears of her life. For years everything had run along smoothly, and she had fulfilled her duty with dedication in a great spirit of obedience. However, it seemed to her now that teaching inside a very beautiful school was no longer appropriate, given what was happening in India and given the missionary spirit that was still alive in her heart.

She asked herself, "What if the Lord wants me to do something else, something more demanding for whoever is suffering in this nation?" Her soul was riddled with doubts. She had reached the moment of crisis. She did not want to admit it, but that was the case.

She decided not to think about it. In two weeks' time, she was leaving to do the Ignatian Spiritual Exercises. She was sure that during that time of silence dedicated to prayer and meditation, clarity would come.

A Spiritual Checkup

The Spiritual Exercises are an annual practice for almost all religious communities and congregations. Once a year male and female religious are invited to leave their work and their living environments to withdraw to a solitary, silent, and meditative location that is suited to reflection and prayer. The Spiritual Exercises were written in the sixteenth century by St. Ignatius of Loyola, the founder of the Society of Jesus, and can be considered a kind of "spiritual checkup" for a person's life. For St. Ignatius, the Spiritual Exercises lasted a month; now they normally last a week. For Sr. Teresa that year, the Spiritual Exercises were supposed to begin on September 12 in Darjeeling, the city in western Bengal where she had spent two years of her novitiate.

Darjeeling is on the slopes of the Himalayas in a very lovely area, dominated by the mountain peak Kanchenjunga, which is higher than 28,000 feet. A health resort built by the English and visited by the wealthy people of Calcutta, Darjeeling in 1946 was a city for the privileged, as it is now, especially in the hot months from May to October. Whoever could afford it came here to flee the muggy and hellish heat of the cities.

The sisters of Our Lady of Loreto went to Darjeeling for their Spiritual Exercises because, apart from fortifying their souls in silence and prayer, they could simultaneously be refreshed physically and enjoy the benefit of the mild and temperate climate.

The Poverty-Stricken Crowd

Sr. Teresa left for Darjeeling the evening of September 10. She had decided to travel at night to avoid the suffocating heat that was quite oppressive during the day. She headed for the station in Calcutta to take a train. A railway line connected the great city on the mouth of the Ganges with the health resort in the Himalayas.

Arriving at the station, Sr. Teresa found herself literally surrounded by a crowd of poverty-stricken people. She was stunned. She had been living in Calcutta for more than sixteen years and knew that it was considered the poverty capital of the world. In no other place on the face of the earth was it possible to find so many poor and dispossessed people.

At other times when she left the school, she had found herself immersed in a swarm of starving and dying people. But that night was different somehow. She seemed to see the reality of it all for the very first time. While she was on her way to the station and while she was waiting for her train, she looked around, worried and almost bewildered. She had the impression that the misery in the city had increased. In addition to the decaying streets, the horrible signs of the recent uprisings were everywhere. Houses were destroyed and half-burnt; thousands of people were camped out in the open, and in that old, deteriorating station, there were innumerable displaced persons—skeletons walking around in hunger and victims of horrible sicknesses. She saw young mothers holding their children and begging for food; groups of children dressed in rags who followed foreigners and asked for food; crippled and blind people sitting on the ground who were pointing to their mouths and asking for something to relieve their hunger pangs.

The train was overcrowded. When it began to move, it did so very slowly so that the people who were crammed in would not fall off the running boards and the roofs of the railway cars.

At every station where the train stopped, the same terrible vision of an immense crowd of skeletal beggars presented itself. Sr. Teresa continued to look around her, shocked. She had never felt so much pity—or so much remorse.

"Children of God"

Sr. Teresa was thinking and reflecting. She was trying to find a possible explanation for so much human pain and misery. Her faith told her that these human skeletons who were traveling with her and who were lingering at the stations were children of God, just as her students at school were. The difference was that she and her students had the good fortune to live comfortably while these children of God were suffering immensely and were deprived of everything. Their lives were worse than that of animals.

She watched the young mothers who held their children to their breasts with infinite tenderness. Their breasts were flat, empty, shriveled—they did not give milk. However, the sentiments of these women were no less noble and no less heartfelt than those of well-to-do women with breasts filled with milk. Their sorrow in seeing their children starving was no less than the sorrow that an American or an English mother would feel.

She was aware of feeling a very great passion for these people. She remembered the gospel. Referring to the poor, Jesus had said, "As you did it to one of the least of these my brethren, you did it to me" (Matthew 25:40). "These" poor people were Jesus, and she, by her religious profession, was the spouse of Jesus. She needed, therefore, to take care of her spouse. She needed to serve "these" poor who were Jesus.

A thousand thoughts crowded Sr. Teresa's mind and heart that night. Little by little, as the train proceeded, it left behind the mugginess of the plain and wended its way toward the refreshing slopes of the Himalayas. Many passengers, lulled by the rolling of the train and the nighttime breeze, had fallen asleep. Sr. Teresa, instead, was fully alert. She felt that something important was happening. In fact, this was the very night she made the decision that would drastically change her life.

The "Call within a Call"

One day I specifically asked her, "What really happened during that train ride to Darjeeling?" Mother Teresa looked at me in silence. I thought she was not going to answer or that she would address the matter with a single phrase or sentence, as she often did. Instead, she shared with me this extraordinary and moving explanation.

"That night," she said, "my eyes opened to the suffering, and I understood the essence of my vocation at its core. I could actually say that I received a new call from God that night—a call within a call. The Lord invited me not to 'change' my status as a sister but to 'modify' it—to make it adhere more closely to the gospel and to the missionary spirit he had given me. It was an invitation to perfect the vocation that I had been given when

I was eighteen. I felt that the Lord was asking me to renounce my quiet life inside my religious community and go out into the streets to serve the poor.

"It was a command. It was not a suggestion or an invitation or a proposal. That night Jesus 'commanded' me leave the convent. It was a very specific command. I was to leave the convent and go live with the poor.

"But it was not the poor in general. He asked me to serve the dispossessed, the poorest of the poor. Those who have nothing and no one. Those whom no one will approach because they are contagious, filthy, and full of germs and parasites. Those who cannot beg for alms because they are naked and do not have even a rag to wear and cannot go out like that. Those who no longer eat and are so debilitated by starvation that they have no strength to chew food. Those who collapse on the street exhausted and emaciated, aware that they are dying. Those who no longer cry because they have no more tears. These are the people that Jesus told me to love during that train ride. I did the Spiritual Exercises in Darjeeling, reflecting on the message I had received, and when I returned to Calcutta, I was determined to change my life."

•

Chapter Sixteen

DRASTIC CHANGES

Sr. Teresa's visit to Darjeeling in September 1946 lasted ten days. They were the most difficult and important days of her life.

She arrived in turmoil because during her trip, so much had happened in her heart. So she began the Spiritual Exercises knowing that she would need to "revolutionize" her life. Jesus' command was, in fact, clear to her. Sr. Teresa needed to decide to leave the religious community she had embraced when she was eighteen to pursue this new vocation. But how would she be able to do it?

Telling the Truth

Leaving the convent meant creating a scandal. She was a well-known and esteemed teacher. What would the other sisters, the students, and their families think? How would they judge her actions?

She did not, of course, want to leave the convent because she was tired of being a sister but because she was called by God to a new spiritual task. The Lord had directed her to fulfill other ideals and objectives. All of it involved activity outside the convent walls. How was she going to explain this to other people?

No Catholic religious community had ever—at least not up until then—set for itself the ideals that Sr. Teresa had in mind. For that reason the new project for her life was original, extraordinary, and unheard of in traditional ecclesiastical groups. She would have to establish a new movement, a new religious family. She would need to become the "foundress" of a new community.

It was a very grand ideal that nevertheless entailed major problems, not only from a practical, organizational, and economic point of view, but also from a juridical and institutional perspective. Throughout history sisters who founded new religious communities almost always had extensive experience with religious life and were of a certain age. They also appeared gifted with particular ascetic charisms of one kind or another.

Sr. Teresa, at age thirty-six, was young and had been in the convent for eighteen years. She had made perpetual vows—a lifelong profession—in 1937, only nine years earlier. As a sister, she had always been a teacher, and no one ever noticed that she might have charismatic gifts. On paper, therefore, she did not have the qualities suitable to engender immediate confidence on the part of her superiors that would lead them to grant her their permission to leave the convent to found a new community.

Furthermore, as a religious she was subject to the Church and bound by perpetual vows. She would not be able to do anything, therefore, without the permission of her ecclesiastical superiors.

The only way for her to leave the convent without breaking off her relationship with the Church was to obtain special authorization from the pope. In addition, she would need several other ecclesiastical permissions to found a new community.

First Sr. Teresa would need to talk to her superior at St. Mary's High School in Calcutta and then the mother general in Dublin. In the meantime she would need to inform the archbishop of Calcutta about her plans because it was up to him to request the necessary authorization from the pope. But what arguments could this young sister use to convince the important authorities?

"I will tell them the truth," she kept saying. The truth was that on a night in September, during a train trip from Calcutta to Darjeeling while she was looking at the poor people traveling with her, Jesus "commanded" her to leave the convent and begin serving the poorest of the poor of the world.

But who would believe her? They would probably take her for an unbalanced mystic or merely a young sister who was tired of doing her duty and looking for a way to escape it. They might judge her desire to serve the poorest of the poor as an excuse to get away from the rigorous routines of the convent and the monotony of daily obedience.

During the Spiritual Exercises, she evaluated and reevaluated all the possibilities. She was perfectly aware that what she wanted to do was very complicated and that her conduct would bring problems for her superiors. She was certain that this whole affair would definitely damage her relationship with the sisters of Our Lady of Loreto. She also began to wonder if perhaps these ideas and aspirations could have come from the devil. Could they be temptations?

She prayed intensely to have a sign—some certitude. She confided in her confessor. She truly felt overwhelmed by this unexpected "calling" that was turning her life upside down.

When she finished the Spiritual Exercises, she returned to Calcutta. During the train ride back, she saw the sea of misery again that was rippling around the periphery of inhabited centers and in the train stations—a sea that slowly increased as she approached the large city. The suffering people looked at her with bewildered eyes, and she felt that she should help them. She felt that she loved them as she had never loved anyone else because she had discovered that they were Jesus.

When she returned to St. Mary's High School, she went back to doing her normal tasks. However, she had already become a different person.

Shock and Fear

At that time preparations for the beginning of the new academic year were in full swing. The girls were coming back from vacation and the school was coming alive again. Work for the sisters and the teachers intensified. Appointments, meetings, decisions, reunions—the flurry of activity took up all her time. Sr. Teresa, however, did not forget about her dilemma.

Mother Teresa told me, "The 'calling' that I felt on the night of September 10 on the train to Darjeeling had all the characteristics of a 'command.' Because of that, I *knew* within myself that I would need to obey. I had no doubts about that, but I did not know *how* I was going to be able to do it."

She knew, though, that she had to act. She had to talk about her plans and assess reactions; she had to recognize the difficulties, discuss them, weigh them, and, in the end, she had to overcome them.

She wanted to confide in someone but immediately understood how complicated the situation was. The first people to whom she timidly and cautiously revealed her aspirations were some of the sisters living with her at St. Mary's High School. They listened to her with perplexity, and as one would expect, they were shocked. Then she turned to the superior of the community. She got the same reaction—and, in fact, a worse one. The superior at St. Mary's High School rushed to refer the matter to the provincial superior who, in turn, immediately informed the archbishop of Calcutta, Archbishop Ferdinand Perier.

As the archbishop recounted later, the sisters were frightened. They told him that a young sister in their community, perhaps exhausted by too much work, had "strange ideas," so he needed to intervene before she could move ahead and cause a scandal. The sisters were thinking about their community and about their school's good name. They were not giving their colleague any credit for her plans or any weight to her spiritual dilemma. On the contrary, they did not consider her point of view at all. In fact, in the report to the archbishop, they took for granted that he, too, would arrive at the same conclusions and that he would take disciplinary measures "against" Sr. Teresa.

The Archbishop's No

Archbishop Perier, however, was a man of great spiritual experience. Guiding the Catholic community in a chaotic city like Calcutta—where all kinds of religions, philosophies, and esoteric and confusing ideas merged and overlapped—was a task that called not only for intelligence, astuteness, and prudence but especially for faith and good instincts. He always needed to be ready to "look" beyond appearances, beyond the surface. Archbishop Perier was well seasoned in this kind of exercise.

He had listened attentively to Mother Superior's report, but he was not worried, let alone shocked. He merely said he wanted to talk to the young sister himself and to hear about her aspirations from her.

That meeting happened during the course of a visit by the archbishop to St. Mary's High School. Archbishop Perier had a long talk with Sr. Teresa, during which he received an excellent impression of her. However, he did not want to express that sentiment. He knew that time is always an important factor for shedding light on spiritual matters. He needed to delay to be able to know God's plan in case this was indeed God's plan.

Mother Teresa told me: "I confided my desire to the bishop. I told him that Jesus asked me to leave the convent of the Loreto sisters to start a new life dedicated to the poorest of the poor. Archbishop Perier listened to me patiently, looking attentively into my eyes, and at the end, he gave me a firm and curt 'No.'"

No one knows what the archbishop related to the superior at St. Mary's High School after his talk, but he certainly did not tell her to "give credence" to Sr. Teresa's desire. That fact solidified the superior's conviction that the young nun was the victim of illusions and fantasies.

A Traitor

Sr. Teresa's difficulties became greater and more serious. By this time, all the religious in the community knew about her plans, but no one paid any attention to them.

Sr. Teresa experienced a great deal of mistrust from the other sisters. They shunned her and stood aloof, almost as if she were a traitor. They also tried to distance the students from her, fearing that she could hurt their formation with her odd ideas. She felt alone and abandoned, so she suffered greatly. She sought comfort in prayer, but her thoughts, worries, and discomfort in the community wore down not only her mind but also her physical health. She lost her appetite, began to suffer insomnia, and increasingly experienced stomach pains and migraines. As her health visibly declined, it became quite clear that she was ill.

The other sisters seemed almost happy about her illness. For them it was "providential." Her illness came just at the right time to resolve a difficult and regrettable situation. It was decided rather suddenly that she should be transferred to another house in the congregation.

This was a question of a "strategic" transfer. From the time Sr. Teresa had revealed her new goals, the provincial superior wanted to distance her from St. Mary's High School, but she did not know how she would justify a transfer to another place because Sr. Teresa was loved and respected by so many people. The "illness" was a golden opportunity, so she immediately took advantage of it. Sr. Teresa understood. This was a punitive transfer, and she thought that she would never again return to her teaching position.

The Superior General

Archbishop Perier was not pleased about the transfer. He was watching over the young sister in whose eyes he had seen great faith in God. When he learned that she had been transferred, even though it was for health reasons, he intervened and had her return to Calcutta to her position at the high school. He decided at that point that the time had come to deal with the entire situation.

Although Sr. Teresa had asked him to allow her to leave the convent so that she could begin serving the poorest of the poor in the city, she did not want her departure to be definitive. She wanted to do a trial run to test her capacity for endurance and the possibility of accomplishing this inspired project. Sr. Teresa demonstrated by this approach that she was prudent and was not letting her enthusiasm control her. The archbishop appreciated her wise balance.

There was another problem, however. The political situation at that time was not conducive to this kind of experiment. India had gained its independence from the English, and a wave of nationalism was moving across that large country. Under Gandhi's inspiration, political and intellectual groups were meeting together to develop social services for the poorest classes. How would they feel if they met a European woman in the slums of Calcutta who wanted to do the same thing? She needed to wait.

Archbishop Perier told Sr. Teresa to be patient. By this time, however, the archbishop believed in the ideals that she wanted to pursue. For that reason he suggested that in the meantime, she should initiate the legal paperwork to obtain permission to live outside the convent.

"I immediately wrote to the motherhouse in Dublin," Mother Teresa told me. "After a few weeks, I received an answer. The mother general was quite sympathetic. 'If the Lord is calling you,' she wrote, 'I authorize you wholeheartedly to leave the community. Remember, no matter what happens, we love you. If you wish to return someday, know that there will always be a place for you.'

"I received approval from Mother General, but I needed authorization from the Holy See. However, that authorization depended on the action of the archbishop. Archbishop Perier was not in a hurry. I met with him often. He would ask me many questions, but he was not fully decided. Finally, on February 2, 1948, he sent a request to the Congregation for Institutes of Consecrated Life, the appropriate office at the Vatican. Four months later, at the beginning of June, the response came. The Congregation authorized me to be a sister living outside the convent. However, I had to continue living according to the Rule of my religious family and in obedience to the archbishop of Calcutta."

A Sister outside the Convent

At the time of this request for paperwork and permissions from superiors, the direct presence of God manifested itself yet another time in a mysterious way, guiding the steps of the young sister.

Sr. Teresa wanted to leave the convent to work among the poor, but she wanted to do it as a sister, maintaining her state of consecration to God through her vows. For that reason she insisted on asking her superiors for "exclaustration," that is, permission to operate outside the convent. Archbishop Perier instead wanted her to ask for "secularization," that is, a return to a lay status. In that case, she would no longer be tied to her vows and would be a completely free agent like other laypeople.

When she wrote to her superior general, Sr. Teresa asked for exclaustration. Archbishop Perier, who read the letter before approving it, made her rewrite it, directing her to ask for secularization instead.

With a heavy heart, she reluctantly obeyed. However, when the answer came, she was very happy to read that the superior general understood her vocation, supported her desire to work outside the convent, but also proposed that she ask the Congregation for exclaustration and not for secularization.

Now she needed to write to Rome. Encouraged by the suggestion of Mother General, she asked again for exclaustration. Once again, the archbishop, firm in his ideas, rejected her letter, saying, "Request secularization or I will not give my approval." Again, suffering with a heavy heart, she obeyed. She rewrote the letter and conformed herself to the will of her ecclesiastical superior.

However, when she got her response, her heart leapt for joy. The Vatican Congregation gave her permission for exclaustration but not for secularization. Thus, she could start a new life outside the convent but remain a sister bound by her vows. This was exactly what she had wanted.

This very significant detail was a new confirmation of God's will. God was guiding her destiny, and she felt peaceful. "I waited another four months to be sure about the step I was going to take," she said. "On August 16, 1948, I put aside the habit of the sisters of Our Lady of Loreto, and I left the convent."

Chapter Seventeen

THE BEGINNING OF THE MISSION

Leaving the community of Our Lady of Loreto was the biggest sacrifice of my life," Mother Teresa informed me. "I suffered a lot when I left my family and my country to enter the convent when I was eighteen. But I suffered much more when I left the convent to begin the new work that Jesus had commanded me to do.

"I had received my spiritual formation from that community. I had become a sister and had consecrated myself to God. I loved the work I was doing at St. Mary's High School in Calcutta. Leaving what had become my second family cost me tremendously.

"When the door of the convent closed behind me on August 16, 1948, and I found myself alone on the streets of Calcutta, I felt a deep sense of loss and almost fear that was difficult to overcome."

The Feast of the Assumption

Sr. Teresa wanted her last day in the convent to be August 15, the Feast of the Assumption. It is a Catholic feast that celebrates one of the most amazing events in history: the bodily assumption of a human being, Mary, the mother of Jesus, into heaven.

According to tradition and confirmed by faith, Our Lady did not die like other human beings at the end of her earthly existence. While she was sleeping, angels came to take her to heaven, where her body is now. Her body was glorified, a pledge of the resurrection of the body that Jesus promises to all. According to other traditions, Our Lady died like all human beings, and her assumption into heaven occurred immediately after her death. In either case, the mother of Jesus is there in that mysterious dimension that we cannot understand but that faith tells us is real: Our Lady is there, body and soul, like Jesus.

The Feast of the Assumption, which dates back in Christian tradition from the seventh century, does not refer merely to a pious belief held for centuries but to a dogma of faith. In 1950 the assumption of Mary into heaven was declared a fundamental truth of the Catholic faith that all must believe in order to fully understand the reality of their lives. But even in 1948, all Catholics knew of its importance and profound significance.

Sr. Teresa, in particular, paid attention to this feast. In her meditations she often lingered over it to understand its meaning more fully. She especially liked to reflect on the fact that it contained very concrete truths about eternal life for the body as well as the soul. No human being was excluded. For Sr. Teresa, this feast highlighted specifically the ideals that she wanted to realize.

Even the innumerable human skeletons that were swarming around the slums of Calcutta would be resurrected one day. Bodies—decomposing, reeking, covered with sores, skeleton-like, ravaged by leprosy and a thousand other diseases—would enter the kingdom of God glorified and splendid and continue to live in the surpassing joy of well-being and happiness. Sr. Teresa was meditating on all of this and said to herself, "It is not a fable. It is a reality won by Christ."

The Catholic Church teaches that the body is the temple of the Holy Spirit. Through his passion and death, Jesus has redeemed human beings—their souls but also their bodies. Sr. Teresa was preparing to serve people whose bodies were often considered revolting, people who had nothing and were worth nothing in the eyes of the world. However, for a believer these people were still children of God. Jesus was hiding himself inside those ravaged bodies.

What Sr. Teresa was to begin was the greatest and most concrete testimony of love and faith that anyone could ever imagine. Her mission of helping and loving people rejected by society was a proclamation of the royal dignity of the human being that remains true even if a person's body is diseased, deformed, or decaying. The body is always the temple of the Holy Spirit, redeemed by Christ and destined for resurrection.

The Saris of the Poor

Jesus' command to her on the night of September 10, 1946, was clear and precise: "Serve the poorest of the poor. Live among them, and live as they live." This was a tremendous ideal that would entail unimaginable sacrifices. It was also an expression of absolute love. Sr. Teresa was revolutionizing her life precisely for that ideal.

First, she would need to choose a habit—one that would reflect the way of life for her and her futures companions. She decided to wear a sari of coarse material, the garment most common in India. She chose white, a nondescript color, bordered with three blue stripes, recalling the color of the sky. For shoes she chose sandals.

The poor she had decided to serve were for the most part people stricken by leprosy and covered with sores. They had a dire need for medical assistance. Therefore, she needed to learn the fundamental aspects of medicine, including how to give injections and to bandage sores. She needed to take nursing classes.

Leaving Calcutta, she went to Patna, on the southern bank of the Ganges River, where the Medical Mission Sisters founded by Mother Anna Dengel were running Holy Family Hospital and offering a nursing course. She asked to be taught about medical practices and attended classes for four months. "She was a highly committed student," the sisters in Patna said later. "In four months she learned what usually takes a year to learn."

Rice and Salt

From that time on, she wanted to live according to the Rule that she would adopt for her community: "to live like the poorest of the poor."

The poor in Bengal ate rice and salt. Sr. Teresa sustained herself at that time with rice seasoned with salt. It was a diet on the edge of sustenance. The sisters intervened firmly. "If you continue doing this, you will be committing a serious sin," they told her. "In a very short time, you will become consumptive and die, and you will not be able to do anything for the poor. If your body is not adequately nourished, it cannot function."

This was rational, commonsense advice. Sr. Teresa reflected on it and realized that she was letting herself get carried away by enthusiasm that could become even fatal for her. These sisters had degrees in medicine and knew their field. She needed to listen to them. She decided that she and her future community would have a diet that was simple but sufficient to keep them healthy enough to work with total dedication in service to the poor.

It needs to be said, however, that the phrase "simple but sufficient" never had the meaning for Mother Teresa and her sisters that we would imagine. It meant nourishing themselves with the bare essentials so that they could still function. It was the nutrition of the poor. I attended lunches and dinners with Mother Teresa and her sisters on some occasions, and I have to say that I did not see much difference between what they ate and what I saw the poor families in India eating.

After four months with Mother Dengel's sisters in Patna, Sr. Teresa decided to return to Calcutta. She thought she had learned at least enough of the fundamentals to offer aid to the sick; the rest she could learn on the job. She was eager to begin serving the poor.

Beginning the Mission

It was December. Christmas was coming soon, and she wanted to begin her mission on the very day of Christmas. This was another symbolic and very significant choice. Her faith in Christ was always applied concretely, objectively, almost physically, so to speak.

Christmas and the assumption are thought-provoking mysteries in Catholicism that forcefully call attention to the fact that human beings consist both of soul and body. For both feasts the emphasis is placed precisely on the body: God manifested himself in a "human body" at Christmas, and the "glorified body" of Mary entered into the eternal dimension at the assumption.

At Christmas the Church remembers the second Person of the Most Holy Trinity, the Son of God who became man, who was born of a woman, who became a baby called Jesus—a baby who was so poor and defenseless that he was born in a manger. This is the beginning of that dramatic and mysterious adventure in which God entered into history. The adventure would culminate with Jesus' passion and death on the cross. This is an incomprehensible tragedy to us, a mystery of absolute love that is called redemption, through which Jesus restored to humanity the dignity of being children of God—a dignity that they had at the beginning but lost through sin.

Because of the redemption of Christ, human beings are children of God. They are, therefore, all brothers and sisters to one another without distinction. The differences that are visible to the world are due to people forgetting about the implications of redemption, because those differences are superficial.

These were the underlying principles of Sr. Teresa's mission. On the night of September 10, 1946, the night of the "call within a call," she had understood this, and on her journey toward its fulfillment, she wanted to continually recall the divine-historical realities that were leading her on her path. Her mission to the poorest of the poor needed to begin, of course, on the day in which the Church celebrates that God, out of love for human beings, became a poor, anonymous, defenseless baby. And that is what happened.

From Heaven to Hell

That morning after Mass, Sr. Teresa went to visit the only slum she knew about, the slums of Moti Jhil that bordered the building of St. Mary's High School where she had taught for so many years. Her students who visited that ghetto once a week had told her so many horrific stories about the people's lives of misery there. Those stories had affected the instinctive generosity of her heart and contributed to the maturing of her new vocation. Although Sr. Teresa had never set foot in that slum during her time in the convent, she now wanted it to become her home.

Throughout Christmas Day she stopped to socialize with the women and children who lived in Moti Jhil. She was happy because she finally felt that she was "home." From now on these people would be her family. She was so happy that she forgot that she did not have a place to sleep that night. As evening approached, she started looking for lodgings. A woman rented her a squalid shack for five rupees a month. That was her first house.

The next day people could hear Sr. Teresa in that shack repeating the beginning letters of the Bengali alphabet; she had already found five children to teach. The hut had no table, no chairs, no blackboard, and no chalk. She traced the letters of the alphabet on the dirt floor with a large stick.

Only a few months earlier, this nun had been the principal at the famous nearby high school that everyone in Calcutta knew about. In that wonderful school, she had taught the daughters of well-to-do families, young girls who would later become teachers and professors. Now she was in the ghetto, where the destitute lived among rats and cockroaches, and was teaching the children of nobodies, children who otherwise would never have learned to read.

In that shack in the middle of that poor slum, the heat was suffocating. It was over 115 degrees and the humidity was over 95 percent. Sr. Teresa's clothes were sticking to her sweaty body, which seemed to have been invaded by filth.

Everything in that ghetto was filthy: the huts, the paths between huts that also served as sewers, the ground, the people, the rags they wore. On the floor of her hut, she saw insects and rats moving around. The children's heads were full of lice. Sr. Teresa remembered the school, her clean room, the fans that cooled the room, the white mosquito nets. It seemed as though she had gone from heaven to hell. But it was precisely in this hell that the poor were living, the beloved brothers and sisters of Jesus that she had chosen to serve. In spite of the filth, she was happy.

The Labyrinth of Poverty in Calcutta

Mother Teresa told me: "The transition was very difficult. In the convent, on a practical level, I lived without any difficulties; I never lacked for anything. Now everything was different. Now I was sleeping on the floor, and at night the hut was infested by mice and rats. I ate what the people I helped ate, and only when there was a bit of food. It was a tremendous change, but it did not weigh on me. I had chosen this life to fulfill the gospel to the letter, especially where it says, 'I was hungry and you gave me food. . . . I was naked and you clothed me. . . . I was in prison and you came to me' [Matthew 25:35, 36]. I was loving Jesus in the poorest of the poor of Calcutta, and when I loved like that, I did not feel the pain and fatigue.

"From the very beginning, I had no time to be bored. In that slum the number of children who gathered around me quickly increased. After three days, five became twenty-five, and by the end of the month, there were forty-one. Some years later, a school was established on that spot by my congregation that accommodates more than five hundred children."

I asked Mother Teresa, "Did you help anyone besides the children at first?"

"As I said," she replied, "Jesus' command concerned the poorest of the poor. Through the children I began to penetrate into the labyrinth of the most squalid poverty in Calcutta.

"At that time there were about one million homeless in the city. I also began to visit other slums. I went from hut to hut to see if I could be useful in some way. I helped those who were sleeping on the sides of the streets who ate from the garbage cans. I encountered the most horrendous suffering—people who were blind, crippled, or suffering from leprosy; people with disfigured faces and deformed bodies; people who could not stand on their own, who followed me on all fours begging for a bit of food.

"One day in a pile of garbage, I found a woman who was half dead. Her body was covered with bites from rats and flies. I carried her to a hospital, but they told me that they would not take her because nothing more could be done for her. I protested that I would not leave if they would not hospitalize her. They discussed it for a long time, and in the end, they accommodated me. The woman recovered. Later, thanking me for what I had done for her, she said, 'And to think that it was my son who threw me into the garbage!' Her statement highlighted the most desecrating and devastating consequences of poverty: the rupture and disintegration of normal affection—even the primal, instinctive affection that binds children to parents.

"Another time I absolutely needed to find a hut to shelter some abandoned people. I walked for hours and hours under a blistering sun in search of one. By nighttime I could barely keep standing, and I was close to fainting from exhaustion. Only then did I understand the exhaustion of the poor, who are always looking for a bit of food or medicine or a roof."

Nothing Left

I asked her, "Were there some events at the beginning of your 'new life' that are particularly memorable?"

"Everything that happened then remains in my heart," she replied. "There were terrible, overwhelming experiences that were impossible to withstand from the human point of view. I was just a woman without experience and without means. I was living in complete abandonment to God, and he was the one guiding me. Otherwise, I could not have endured the ordeal. I felt the presence of God every moment during those days, and I can attest to his continual intervention.

"One day while I was walking the streets of Calcutta, a priest approached me and asked me to contribute to a worthy cause. That morning I had left the house with all the money I had—five rupees. During the day I had spent four rupees on the poor. Until some help arrived, I had only one rupee to live on. Trusting in God, I gave my last rupee to that priest. In my mind I prayed, 'Lord, I have nothing left, so you need to take care of that.' Toward evening a person I did not know came to my door. He gave me an envelope and said, 'This is for your work.'

"I was surprised because I had begun my apostolate only a few days earlier, and no one knew me yet. Who could that person have been? I opened the envelope and found fifty rupees. I had the distinct impression that God had wanted to give me a tangible sign of affirmation for all that I was doing. That sum represented a wealth of riches to me. Those rupees were like a note from heaven that said, 'Be strong and keep moving forward!'"

•

Chapter Eighteen

THE MISSIONARIES OF CHARITY

From time to time, Sr. Teresa met some of her former students in the Moti Jhil slums. They were still coming to help the poor. There was, however, a difference. Her former students were visiting the poor and then returning to their comfortable homes. Sr. Teresa was living with the poor and like the poor. She had become one of them.

Significant Sacrifices

Her former students looked at her with admiration but also with dismay. They would stop to talk to her and help her, especially in caring for children, but they were dumbfounded and perplexed when they thought about the way of life she had chosen. They could not quite understand the reason for so much dedication and sacrifice on her part. They felt that she could have helped the poor people while continuing to teach at the high school.

One of the young women, however, felt an attraction to her choice. After all, Sr. Teresa had flung herself into a heroic enterprise, and heroism is always appealing to young people. However, Sr. Teresa's personal example and the lifestyle that would distinguish her future religious community were definitely daunting. She was leading a life of total physical and moral sacrifice. Who could find the strength to be like that?

Mother Teresa said to me one day, "Love, when it is genuine and profound, can do all things." She added, "Certain sacrifices can only be done through love."

The solitude in her new work weighed heavily on her. Sr. Teresa prayed for the Lord to send some companions. "You commanded me to leave the convent and entrusted this new mission to me," she said to Jesus. "It is up to you to find co-workers for me if you want to see what you have asked for come to pass."

The First "Daughter"

At the beginning of 1949, a young woman came to her door who would be her first spiritual "daughter," the first sister of her community. Her name was Subhasini Das, and she was twenty-five years old. She belonged to a well-to-do family and had been a student at St. Mary's High School. She wanted to leave everything behind and follow the example of her former teacher.

"When this young girl told me of her desire," Mother Teresa said, "my heart skipped a beat. I felt a great tenderness and great gratitude toward her, and I looked at her incredulously. I had been alone since I had started my new life. I had no one with whom I could share my plans, my aspirations, my ideas. I unburdened myself to Jesus and prayed, but I really wanted to have someone alongside me. I missed the sisters in the convent. When solitude is absolute, it becomes crushing, so being able to have a companion who wanted to share my ideals filled me with joy.

"However, it was important not to be hasty. I thought about the caution that the archbishop of Calcutta, Archbishop Perier, had exercised toward me when I had asked to change my life.

Therefore, I told Subhasini, 'You need to think very carefully about this because what you are asking to do is very demanding. You could regret it.' The young woman replied, 'I have already considered that.'

"I wanted to throw my arms around her and say, 'Well, in that case, come live with me,' but I stopped myself. I reflected for a few moments and then said, 'Go home and pray for now. Come back to me in a few months, on the Feast of St. Joseph.'

"That date was about three months away. I thought that it would be enough time for Subhasini to see very clearly what was in her heart. If she came back, it would mean that it was a genuine call from the Lord."

In the meantime, Sr. Teresa continued her apostolate in the slums. She worked with the poor every day, but at night she was now staying with the Little Sisters of the Poor, a congregation that cares for the elderly poor.

Then a Belgian Jesuit, Fr. Celeste Van Exem, the rector of the church of Our Lady of Sorrows who knew Sr. Teresa well and was following her activity discretely, found her some decent lodging. She was given a couple of rooms on the second floor of a modest house where the family of Michael Gomes lived. Gomes was Sr. Teresa's first significant benefactor.

In February 1949 she moved into that small house. She was still alone. Every so often, though, she was visited by a widow who did housecleaning at the school where she had taught, and she would spend a few hours in this woman's company. She was the only one who was reaching out in friendship to Sr. Teresa at that time.

Sr. Teresa had set up her bed in the smallest of the rooms at her disposal from Michael Gomes. She transformed the largest one, the one at the top of the stairs that led to the third floor, into a small chapel.

With the help of some young men, she built a small wooden altar on which she placed a picture of the Immaculate Heart of Mary, a gift from Fr. Van Exem. She had prayed often before this altar during the most difficult days. For that reason she wanted the picture in the chapel. (Later she always took the picture with her. It is now in the chapel of the motherhouse of her community.)

She lived alone in this small house for a whole month. Then her first companion arrived on March 19, 1949, the Feast of St Joseph. Sr. Teresa got up early as usual and was getting ready to go to the slums. She heard someone knock at the door. When she opened it, there stood her delicate-looking former student, Subhasini Das.

The Family Grows

"Mother," said the young woman, "today is the Feast of St. Joseph, and I have come back to be with you forever."

Subhasini Das called her "Mother" and not "Professor" or "Sister," as she had done at the high school. She called her "Mother" because in choosing to follow this nun in her venture, she had become her spiritual daughter. Subhasini was aware that she was the first of a number of "daughters" who would soon arrive.

Hearing herself called by that name, Sr. Teresa experienced great consolation. She also sensed the historic significance of that moment and of that name. She sensed in that moment that her family was beginning to exist concretely—the family that would later be called the Missionaries of Charity.

Subhasini Das exchanged her elegant sari for a poor one like Mother Teresa's. She also changed her name. Out of affection for her former teacher, with whom she was now a co-worker, she chose the name that Mother Teresa had as a girl: Agnes.

Mother Teresa's plan was starting to become a reality, and Agnes was the first building block. A second young woman arrived the following week who was also one of Mother Teresa's former students. In May a third one arrived. In a letter to a friend in Europe, Mother Teresa wrote: "You will be pleased to know that I have three companions who are hardworking and full of zeal. We visit five slums, where we go for a few hours. How much suffering! How much need for God! We are still so few in number to bring our Lord to them. You should see the faces of the people light up when the sisters arrive. They may be filthy and naked, but they have hearts full of love. I rely on your prayers. Ask Our Lady to send more sisters. Even if there were twenty of us, there would be work enough for everyone just in Calcutta alone."

Mother Teresa was in a hurry. The work she had undertaken on behalf of the poor required many workers. Since it was crushing work, it was not easy to find young people ready to make so many sacrifices. Six months after Subhasini Das's arrival, Mother Teresa had four companions.

It was a slow increase, but Mother Teresa made great plans anyway. She wrote in a letter in November 1949: "Pray fervently so that our small group grows. There are five of us now, but, God willing, others will join us, and then we will be able to set up a ring of charity around Calcutta and use our centers in the various slums as points from which the love of our Lord can freely shine forth into this city."

She had a grand plan in mind, but at that point, she was focused only on Calcutta. She certainly could not have imagined that one day her sisters would be stationed throughout the world.

Meanwhile, she also succeeded in finding some collaboration from laypeople. She had organized medical dispensaries in the slums where some young Catholic doctors and nurses were helping her care for the sick. She had succeeded in having a Sunday Mass reserved in the parish in the area for the children of the slums. "We took the children and their mothers to church," she wrote in November 1949 to a friend in Europe. "There were 300 children and 120 mothers. A few months ago in May, there were only 26."

The Rule

Her small community continued to grow. There were six young sisters, then seven, then ten. The archbishop of Calcutta was monitoring the development of this spiritual enterprise from a distance.

Now that Mother Teresa had a group of followers, she could ask Rome for official permission to found a new congregation. She could take the first step to obtain initial legal recognition. However, she needed to present Rome with a detailed document, a "constitution" for the new congregation, a document in which the ideals and the rules of the new religious congregation were spelled out in a clear and concise way.

She got to work. Everything was clear in her mind because when Jesus called her, he had explained to her precisely what he wanted her to do. At night when her companions were sleeping, Mother Teresa would pray in her small room and take notes to prepare a constitution.

Here are some excerpts from the document. One sees a continual repetition of the firm commitment to the fundamental concept of her initiative—to serve the poorest of the poor:

Our object is to quench the thirst of Jesus Christ on the cross by dedicating ourselves freely to serve the poorest of the poor, according to the work and teaching of Our Lord, thus announcing the Kingdom of God in a special way.

Our special mission is to work for the salvation and holiness of the poorest of the poor. As Jesus was sent by the Father, so he sends us, full of his Spirit, to proclaim the gospel of his love and pity among the poorest of the poor throughout the world.

Our special task will be to proclaim Jesus Christ to all peoples, above all to those who are in our care. We call ourselves the Missionaries of Charity.

"God is love." The missionary must be a missionary of love, must always be full of love . . . and must also spread it to the souls of others, whether Christian or not.

Bearers of Charity

The plan Mother Teresa wanted to entrust to her religious community through the Rule and its constitution is strictly evangelical. It is based on the fundamental teaching of Christ, which is his teaching about love. It has an ecumenical tone, so it embraces the whole world, Christian and non-Christian, because Christ's salvific love is universal.

Love, understood as "charity" in the gospel sense, is the distinctive element of Mother Teresa's sisters. In fact, they call themselves the "Missionaries of Charity." At an earlier time, Mother Teresa had wanted a different name for her congregation, a name that would make the concept of "bearers of the charity of Christ to the slums" more explicit. Later she chose the name the "Missionaries of Charity" because it is a more concise and less restrictive name.

To live in the command of love intensely and concretely meant that the sisters had to make a special vow at the time of their profession. In addition to the three traditional vows of poverty, chastity, and obedience common to all religious congregations, Mother Teresa wanted them to consecrate themselves to God with an extra vow of "poverty" that is based in charity.

As Mother Teresa explained to me, "With that vow we take on wholehearted and free service to the destitute. This vow means we cannot work for wealthy people, and we cannot accept any recompense for the work we do."

In terms of their religious habit, she decided to adopt the Indian sari that she and the sisters were already wearing: a white sari of coarse material with three blue stripes. The saris were fastened on the left shoulder with a crucifix held by a safety pin to remind the sisters of the cross that Jesus carried.

"The saris," she told me, "allow the sisters to feel poor among the poor, to identify themselves with the sick, with babies, and with elderly abandoned people. Wearing this habit, they share the same way of life as the poor in this world."

The Pope's Approval

Mother Teresa presented her constitution to the archbishop of Calcutta, who examined it carefully. He had his experts look at it and then sent it on to Rome. On October 7, 1950, approval arrived from the Vatican. The congregation was now officially constituted.

"October 7 was a great day for us," she said. "It marked the official, legal beginning of our congregation. I was very happy that the document from Rome arrived that very day, on the Feast of Our Lady of the Rosary. The coincidence seemed to be a sign from heaven. That morning Archbishop Perier came to celebrate Mass in our small chapel, and during the service, Fr. Celeste Van Exem read the document that had come from Rome.

"From that time the community continued to grow. We opened other houses in Calcutta. Canon law states that a new religious institute cannot expand beyond the diocese in which it has begun for ten years. As soon as that period had passed, we began to open houses in other cities in India.

"When a new religious institute is granted the approval of the diocesan bishop after receiving a 'Nulla Osta' ('No Impediments') from the Congregation of Religious Institutes, it is said in legal terms to become 'of diocesan right.' In other words, it has completed the first important step for expansion. If it continues to grow, it can try to obtain the 'Decretum Laudis' ('Decree of Praise') from the pope, allowing expansion anywhere. However, in general the approval for a congregation to be 'of pontifical right' comes only after many years, and sometimes after decades. The Lord was very generous to us. We had waited only fifteen years when Pope Paul VI gave us pontifical approval on February

1, 1965. In that very same year, we opened our first houses outside of India—in Cocorote in the Diocese of Barquisimeto, Venezuela. After that, we opened houses in many other parts of the world.

"Jesus was with us and helped us bring to pass the 'command' that he had given me on the night of September 10, 1946."

•

Chapter Nineteen

AN ARMY THAT
DEFIES THE IMPOSSIBLE

During the centenary of Mother Teresa's birth, the whole world held commemorative events. That year was also the sixtieth anniversary of the first approval for Mother Teresa's Missionaries of Charity ("diocesan right" on October 7, 1950) and the forty-fifth anniversary of the definitive approval ("pontifical right" by Pope Paul VI on February 1, 1965). For Mother Teresa's sisters, 2010 was a special year.

As of 2010, the Missionaries of Charity consisted of 4,500 sisters who worked in 133 countries. It is a large, complex enterprise that requires a lot of work as well as a great deal of economic support. The daughters of Mother Teresa are called upon to face enormous economic problems every day for their own daily lives but especially to maintain their mission to tens of thousands of the poor. They do so relying only on Providence.

Unlike all other religious organizations of men and women who make vows of poverty, chastity, and obedience, the Missionaries of Charity take a fourth vow that particularly characterizes their mission as they commit to "wholehearted service freely given to the poor." The words "freely given" mean they cannot receive fixed compensation for their work. These sisters, therefore, have no stipends of any kind whatsoever, either as individuals or as a group. They constitute an army that cares for an enormous number of the poor, the homeless, the sick, and the needy, and the sisters have no guaranteed funds of any kind. They have only an absolute trust in Divine Providence. From the human point of view, this is an extremely precarious situation—and could even be called a fool-hardy one. Whenever I shared that observation with her, Mother Teresa would always respond by saying, "God wanted this religious congregation, so it is up to him to take care of it."

A Revolution of Love

Mother Teresa went to heaven on September 5, 1997, but she continues to live through each of her sisters. She has transmitted to them a forceful spirituality that is like the wind—a restless, revolutionary wind, a wind of absolute love. Mother Teresa's sisters live by love; they burn with love. They could not remain in the Missionaries of Charity if they did not have that powerful passion.

As we know, genuine love is contagious; it is irresistible. Mother Teresa gave birth to a movement that is similar to the one St. Francis of Assisi began—a movement with universal appeal. It involves not only Christians but also people who allow themselves to "catch" its spirit. It rises beyond religious faiths, ideologies, races, or social categories. It represents the kind of orientation that cuts across and goes beyond all human barriers, traditions, and customs to unite people's hearts. It is a love that is grounded in God, who is love, and that extends to all creatures, especially those who are the neediest and most forgotten. Mother Teresa was pierced by that love the night of September 10, 1946, while on a train to Darjeeling from Calcutta, and it was the beginning of a revolution that is still taking place.

An Ecumenical Movement

Mother Teresa's movement has become more organized as time has gone on. At its beginning, it was just Mother Teresa and a few companions. Today it has become an army and, like other armies, it has various units assigned to carry out different tasks.

Several times Mother Teresa insisted to me that her sisters were not, contrary to appearances, "sisters of the active life" but "contemplatives who live in the midst of the world." Having experienced that the life of prayer is more important than activity and that prayer is the "true lifeline of activity," she wanted to divide her sisters into two groups: an "active branch," dedicated to the exclusive service of the poorest of the poor, and a "contemplative branch," dedicated to that activity for only part of the day. This latter group provides the fundamental support for the "active branch." She wanted the same division in the male branch of her congregation, the Missionaries of Charity Brothers.

Other groups are also part of her movement now. The Missionaries of Charity Fathers are the priests in her congregation. Then there are lay missionaries, men and women who live the same kind of life as the sisters and brothers but who can also marry and have families. These laypeople either associate themselves directly with the apostolate of the Missionaries of Charity, or they find another apostolate that allows them to live out the fourth vow of "wholehearted service freely given to the poor" that Mother Teresa wanted. There are also volunteers, those who share the same vision as that of the Missionaries of Charity and want to live "radiating the love of God" in voluntary poverty, sacrificing all the luxuries of life. They work alongside the actual members of the congregation, and their lives are characterized by prayer and a spirit of service to their families and the community. They can belong to any religion.

Finally, Mother Teresa's great army is rounded out by the "Sick and Suffering Co-Workers" who offer their suffering for the poor and for the work of the Missionaries of Charity. Mother Teresa deeply respected the assistance of these people. She herself, as she told me, was "paired up" with a paralyzed Belgian lady to whom she turned when she was facing particularly difficult problems.

This concept of collaboration is based on the doctrine of the "Mystical Body of Christ," which is the Church. It is one body whose head is Jesus, and we are its members. The members work in harmony and help one another. In line with this truth, the Church has proclaimed St. Thérèse of the Child Jesus, a cloistered Carmelite who lived behind the wall of her convent, the "Patron of Missions." Her heart was full of passionate missionary fire and she prayed, suffered, and offered sacrifices to God for mission work, thus becoming in the eyes of God a genuine and very active missionary.

Mother Teresa's army today is a silent, humble army. During her lifetime Mother Teresa was one of the most well-known people in the world, but she was the most humble person one could ever meet. Her army moves, lives, and acts among the layers of humanity in silence, but its spirit is contagious. Whoever approaches a representative of this army with an open spirit becomes involved. In many Italian parishes, there are groups of young people who volunteer in the name of Mother Teresa because of her example. They do not know each other because they are not seeking publicity, but these small groups are extremely valuable to society.

An Example Who Attracts Others

At the beginning of March 2010, a festival dedicated to Mother Teresa took place in Japan. Catholics are a very small minority in Japan, but Mother Teresa is known in that country. The festival in honor of the centenary of her birth consisted of seven films that illustrated her life and work. The films were shown at the Metropolitan Museum of Photography in the middle of Tokyo. The initial invitations were sent to a few Catholics asking them to bring their non-Catholic friends. The result was simply overwhelming. More than 15,000 people came to see the films. The showings had to be repeated throughout the rest of the month. The festival in Tokyo then moved to other cities in Japan.

The news agency Asia News, which is always very attentive to Christian events in the East, catalogued the reaction of different non-Catholics who attended the festival, and their testimonies are extremely significant; they indicate that it is almost impossible to resist the charismatic attraction that radiates from Mother Teresa. Here are some of their statements:

Haruki Tsukihand, age forty: "Christianity always seemed to me to be an 'upper-class' religion, as if it had a wall all around it. Mother Teresa's example made me understand that Christianity is completely different than what I thought."

Sachiyo Hattori, Shintoist, age fifty: "I thought love was a strange and unattainable idea. Now I know what it means. It means not just talking about it, but acting on behalf of whoever one loves."

Yuko Kataoka (no age listed): "I have known about Mother Teresa's work for some time, but I learned a lot watching the films. Her love was action that became prayer. She made a decision and then followed through. I would like to be able to act as she did."

Hiroyuki Mijake, age thirty-one: "The thing that most surprised me is that Mother Teresa, through her life, transformed an ideology into a reality. It is wonderful to have lived during her lifetime. I am considering the idea of getting baptized because her example is too strong to ignore."

The saying *"Verba volant, exempla trahunt"* ("Words fly away, but examples inspire") has always found a surprising demonstration in relation to Mother Teresa. Considering the fascination—and especially the "character" of the fascination—that this woman has exerted on the world when she was alive and continues to exert through her memory and through the movement she began, one can say that she has been and continues to be one of the most important historical figures of our time. Because of that, the Catholic Church has already proclaimed her "Blessed," and we can imagine that before long the Church will assign her the title of "Saint."

Biographical Timeline

1910, August 26
Mother Teresa is born in Skopje, an Albanian city in Kosovo that later became part of Yugoslavia. She is born into a well-to-do Catholic family. Nikola Bojaxhiu, her father, is a businessman and building contractor. Her mother, Drana, is a beautiful young woman. They already have two children, Aga and Lazar. She is given the name "Agnes" at her baptism, but the family calls her "Gonxha," which means "flower bud" in Albanian.

1919, June
Nikola Bojaxhiu dies at the age of forty-six. He was a city councilman in Skopje and was part of the movement for the annexation of Skopje to Albania. It appears he was poisoned by the Yugoslavian police.

1922
Agnes hears some preaching in her church parish by Jesuit missionaries who are working in India, and for the first time, she experiences a desire to dedicate her life to God and become a missionary. She does not want to become a sister, however, so she lets the voice fade.

1928
At the age of eighteen, Agnes finishes school and thinks about her future. Reading the letters that the missionary Jesuits send from Bengal, she hears the inner voice inviting her again to be a missionary in India, and this time she begins to consider it. However, the only way open to her to realize her dream is to

join a religious community. She joins the community of Our Lady of Loreto because they do mission work in Bengal.

1928, September 25

Agnes leaves her family and goes to Dublin, Ireland, to the motherhouse of Our Lady of Loreto. After a brief stay, she leaves for India on December 1.

1929, January

Arriving in Calcutta, Agnes goes on to Darjeeling, the city on the slopes of the Himalayas where the community of Our Lady of Loreto has a house for novices. She officially begins religious life, receiving the habit and taking the name "Sister Teresa" out of devotion to St. Thérèse of the Infant Jesus.

1931, January 24

After two years of her novitiate, Sr. Teresa makes her simple vows. She leavers Darjeeling for her new assignment at St. Mary's High School, run by her community in Calcutta, to teach history and geography.

1934, May 24

Sr. Teresa makes perpetual vows and becomes the principal of St. Mary's High School.

1946, September 10

On a train trip to Darjeeling to do the Ignatian Spiritual Exercises, Sr. Teresa is unexpectedly struck by the condition of absolute misery of the poverty-stricken people she sees all around her. She experiences a "command" from Jesus Christ and feels a call to leave her community to dedicate herself entirely to the service of the poorest of the poor.

1946, October
Retuning to Calcutta, Sr. Teresa confides her desire to the mother superior, who thinks her plans are absurd. Sr. Teresa continues to believe her inspiration is from God, but she encounters hostility and distrust from her community. Suffering from that reaction, she becomes sick. Archbishop Perier of Calcutta senses that this sister is meant to fulfill a great plan from Providence and decides to help her.

1948, February 2
After examining Sr. Teresa's ideas at length, Archbishop Perier writes to Pope Pius XII requesting "secularization" for the sister who wants to begin her new work outside the convent.

1948, June 6
The Holy See responds to Archbishop Perier's letter and grants "exclaustration" rather than the "secularization" he had requested. Sr. Teresa now has permission to remain a sister while living outside the convent.

1948, August 16
Sr. Teresa lays aside the habit of the community of Our Lady of Loreto and leaves the convent.

1948, September
Sr. Teresa goes to Patna to the hospital of the Medical Missionary Sisters to take a nursing course that will prepare her to better serve the poorest of the poor to whom she is dedicating her life.

1948, December
Sr. Teresa returns to Calcutta and chooses December 25, Christmas Day, as the first day to begin her service to the poorest of the poor.

1949, March 19
On the Feast of St. Joseph, Sr. Teresa's first companion arrives. Subhasini Das, who takes as her religious name "Agnes," is the first sister of the future congregation. Sr. Teresa becomes a spiritual "Mother."

1950, January
Mother Teresa now has ten companions working with her. On the advice of Archbishop Perier, she writes the Rule for the congregation that she is forming. The archbishop examines the document and sends it to Rome.

1950, October 7
News arrives of the Vatican's approval for the new congregation of the Missionaries of Charity.

1952
Mother Teresa founds her first major house of social services, Nirmal Hriday, the Home for the Dying Destitute.

1954
She founds Shishu Bhavan, the Home for Children.

1956
She founds Shanti Naghar, the village for those with leprosy.

1960, October
Mother Teresa leaves India for the first time and goes to America for a conference. On her return she stops in Rome, and, through the assistance of Cardinal Gregorio Agagianian, her request for the Missionaries of Charity to become a congregation of pontifical right is presented to Pope John XXIII.

1962, September
Mother Teresa's work continues to grow and elicits great admiration. The president of India awards her the Padma Shri prize, and the president of the Philippines awards her the Magsaysay Prize.

1963, March 25
The archbishop of Calcutta approves the male branch of Mother Teresa's work, the Missionaries of Charity Brothers.

1964, December
Pope Paul VI meets Mother Teresa during his trip to Bombay. To express his esteem and admiration, he donates to her the luxury car he had used for his meetings throughout India.

1965, February 1
Pope Paul VI grants the pontifical right to Mother Teresa's congregation.

1965, July 26
Mother Teresa goes to Cocorote, Venezuela, and founds her first house outside of India.

1967, December 8
She opens a house in Colombo, Sri Lanka.

1968, August 22
She opens her first center in Rome.

1968, September 8
She opens a house in Tabora, Tanzania.

1969, March 26
Pope Paul VI approves the International Association of the Co-Workers of Mother Teresa.

1969, September 13
Mother Teresa opens a center for Aborigines in Bourke, Australia.

1970, July 16
She opens a house in Amman, Jordan.

1970, December 8
She opens a novitiate house for the Missionaries of Charity in London.

1971, January 6
She receives the Pope John XXIII Peace Prize in Rome from Pope Paul VI.

1971, September
She receives the Good Samaritan Award in Boston, Massachusetts.

1971, October
She opens a house in Belfast, Northern Ireland, and one in the Bronx, New York.

1972, September 15
Mother Teresa receives the Jawaharlal Nehru Prize for International Understanding from the government of India.

1973, April 25
Prince Philip of England confers on Mother Teresa the Templeton Prize for the Promotion of Religion.

1973, October 20
Mother Teresa takes part in a solidarity march in Milan, Italy, and receives the Ambrogino d'Oro, a gold medal, from the mayor.

1975, December 29
Time magazine has a drawing of Mother Teresa on its cover with this inscription: "Living Saints: Messengers of Love and Hope."

1976, January 17
Mother Teresa is on the cover of *Paris Match*, a French weekly magazine.

1976, August 6
Mother Teresa gives a speech in Philadelphia, Pennsylvania, at the 41st International Eucharistic Congress.

1979, March 1
President Sandro Pertini of Italy presents Mother Teresa with the international Balzan Prize for 1978.

1979, October 17
Mother Teresa receives the Nobel Peace Prize in Oslo, Norway.

1980, January 25
She receives the highest civilian award of India, the Bharat
Ratna (Jewel of India).

1981, May
The Faculty of Medicine at the Catholic University of the
Sacred Heart in Milan grants her an honorary medical degree.

1983, August
She is hospitalized and given a pacemaker.

1988, February
She goes to Moscow to get permission from the Communist
government to open a house in the Soviet capital.

1990, March
After repeated heart attacks, Mother Teresa tenders her
resignation as superior general of her congregation. In
September, however, the general chapter meeting of the
congregation unanimously reelects Mother Teresa as superior
and she accepts.

1991, March
Mother Teresa returns to her native country, Albania, and
takes part in the ceremony for the reopening of the cathedral
in Tirana, which had been made into a theater during the
Communist regime. She opens three houses for charitable
works in that country.

1992

Mother Teresa meets Princess Diana, the wife of Prince Charles of England, in Calcutta. Diana was going through a difficult period in her life, and Mother Teresa invites her to dedicate herself to volunteer work. A friendship is established between the two women.

1993

Mother Teresa contracts malaria in India. When she later has another serious heart attack, she is hospitalized in the Birla Heart Research Centre in Calcutta. She is given a second pacemaker.

1996, May 21

She is made an Honorary Citizen of Rome by Mayor Francesco Rutelli at the Campidoglio in Rome.

1996, August 20

Mother Teresa is hospitalized in the Woodlands Hospital in Calcutta after yet another heart attack. Doctors discover that she still tests positive for the malaria she had contracted in 1993.

1996, November 26

Speaking from a hospital in Calcutta after one more heart attack, she says, "Let me die in peace like my destitute people."

1996, November 29

Mother Teresa receives a heart operation with angioplasty in New Delhi.

1997, March
For the third time, Mother Teresa tenders her resignation as superior general of the congregation. The community accepts it and elects Sr. Nirmala Joshi in her place.

1997, June
Mother Teresa and Princess Diana meet in the Bronx, New York, for their last time together.

1997, June 29
Mother Teresa meets Pope John Paul II in Rome for the last time.

1997, September 1
Mother Teresa hears the news about the tragic death of Diana and expresses great sorrow and offers prayers for the princess.

1997, September 5
At 9:30 p.m., while she is preparing to go to bed in the General House in Calcutta, Mother Teresa has her last heart attack and dies.

1997, September 6
News of Mother Teresa's death is reported worldwide. The world grieves profoundly.

1997, September 7
Before his televised recitation of the Angelus from Castel Gandolfo, Pope John Paul II commemorates Mother Teresa, calling her, among other things, "a very dear sister," and pointing to her as an "eloquent example" for believers.

1997, September 9
Cardinal Joseph Ratzinger, during a press conference, also speaks of Mother Teresa and says, "I believe that in Mother Teresa's case, the process of beatification can go forward in an expedited manner since her life was so transparent and luminous."

1997, September 13
Mother Teresa's state funeral is televised throughout the world with heads of states, royalty, and important representatives from many nations in attendance. In the afternoon her body is entombed in the General House of her congregation in Calcutta.

1998, September 5
A young woman in India, an animist, Monica Besra, who was stricken with a serious tumor, invokes Mother Teresa's help and is suddenly healed.

1999, July 26
The process of beatification for Mother Teresa begins. According to canon law, this process can begin only after five years have passed since the death of that person. However, Pope John Paul II makes an exception for Mother Teresa.

2001, July 14
Cardinal Henry S. D'Souza, the archbishop of Calcutta, announces that the diocesan process for beatification is completed.

2002, October
The Vatican Congregation for the Causes of Saints approves Mother Teresa's life of extraordinary moral virtue and the miracle from her intercession.

2002, December 20
Pope John Paul II solemnly promulgates the decrees regarding Mother Teresa's life of heroic virtue and the miracle from her intercession.

2003, October 19
Pope John Paul II celebrates the solemn ceremony of beatification of Mother Teresa in St. Peter's Square with more than 300,000 people in attendance.

the**WORD**
among us®
The *Spirit* of Catholic Living

This book was published by The Word Among Us. For nearly thirty years, The Word Among Us has been answering the call of the Second Vatican Council to help Catholic laypeople encounter Christ in the Scriptures—a call reiterated recently by Pope Benedict XVI and a Synod of Bishops.

The name of our company comes from the prologue to the Gospel of John and reflects the vision and purpose of all of our publications: to be an instrument of the Spirit, whose desire it is to manifest Jesus' presence in and to the children of God. In this way, we hope to contribute to the Church's ongoing mission of proclaiming the gospel to the world and growing ever more deeply in our love for the Lord.

Our monthly devotional magazine, *The Word Among Us*, features meditations on the daily and Sunday Mass readings, and currently reaches more than one million Catholics in North America each year and another 500,000 Catholics in 100 countries. Our press division has published nearly 200 books and Bible studies over the past 12 years.

To learn more about who we are and what we publish, log on to our Web site at **www.wau.org**. There you will find a variety of Catholic resources that will help you grow in your faith.

Embrace His Word, Listen to God . . .

www.wau.org